A Laboratory Course in

Second Edition

C++ Data Structures

James Robergé
Illinois Institute of Technology

Stefan Brandle
Taylor University

David Whittington
Taylor University

JONES AND BARTLETT PUBLISHERS
Sudbury, Massachusetts
BOSTON   TORONTO   LONDON   SINGAPORE

World Headquarters
Jones and Bartlett Publishers
40 Tall Pine Drive
Sudbury, MA 01776
978-443-5000
info@jbpub.com
www.jbpub.com

Jones and Bartlett Publishers
Canada
2406 Nikanna Road
Mississauga, ON L5C 2W6
CANADA

Jones and Bartlett Publishers
International
Barb House, Barb Mews
London W6 7PA
UK

Library of Congress Cataloging-in-Publication Data

Robergé, Jim.
  A laboratory course in C++ data structures / James Robergé, Stefan Brandle, David Whittington.
    p. cm.
  ISBN 0-7637-1976-5
    1. C++ (Computer program language) I. Brandle, Stefan. II. Whittington, David. III.
  Title.

  QA76.73.C153R58 2003
  005.13'3–dc21

                                                                        2002044401

Editor-in-Chief, College: J. Michael Stranz
Production Manager: Amy Rose
Associate Editor: Theresa DiDonato
Associate Production Editor: Karen C. Ferreira
Production Assistant: Jenny L. McIsaac
Senior Marketing Manager: Nathan J. Schultz
Composition: Northeast Compositors
Cover Design: Night & Day Design
Manufacturing Buyer: Therese Bräuer
Printing and Binding: Courier Stoughton
Cover Printing: Courier Stoughton

Printed in the United States of America
07 06 05 04 03   10 9 8 7 6 5 4 3 2 1

To my son Edward, who lets me see a world of wonder through his eyes. And to my wife, Ruby, who creates that world.

—James Robergé

To Christina, Anna, and Esther: my queen and little princesses.

—Stefan Brandle

In memory of my kitty Sweetpea.

—David Whittington

Preface to the Second Edition

We have used James Robergé's laboratory manual for three years at Taylor University. The approach and style of the original manual made it an extremely effective teaching tool. It has been central to our data structures courses, but aspects of it are now out of date because of changes in the C++ language. Our goal in creating this revision was not to deviate from Robergé's original vision of the laboratory experience, which he developed through considerable experimentation and refinement, but rather, to provide an update to the material presented throughout the labs. Significant modifications have been made to reflect changes in the C++ language and current common object-oriented practices. We have also added some new material and made some changes to the content and ordering of material in an attempt to make it easier to pair this laboratory manual with existing textbooks.

Overview of Changes

The code has been updated to comply with ANSI C++ standards. This includes the following changes:

- Error handling is now performed using exception, instead of assert, statements. Assert statements are still discussed. They are not, however, used in the source code included in the book or on the Web.
- All header files have been changed from the now deprecated <*.h> to the modern ANSI C++ <*>.
- The standard namespace is used in all appropriate places.

The coding style has been updated to fall in line with practices common to modern object-oriented languages. The following changes have been made:

- Functions that return Boolean values are prefaced with 'is'.
- Functions that in some way interact with and return private data from within a class are now prefaced with 'get'.
- Functions that are passed values used to set private data in a class are now prefaced with 'set'.

The order and pace of the information presented has been changed to follow available textbooks more closely.

- Dynamic memory allocation has been removed from the point list lab and is now introduced starting with Lab 3, the array based list.
- Templates are now introduced with Lab 5, the stack ADT.
- The string, heap, and performance evaluation labs are no longer included as part of the recommended lab order. They are, however, still included in order to provide material for multi-quarter and multi-semester courses, as optional homework assignments, and for those who wish to use them in the place of standard labs.
- Two labs have been added: "Lab 8: Copying and Comparing ADTs"—which covers data structure assignment and comparison operators, and copy and convert constructors—and "Lab 14: The Hash Table ADT".

Note: We do not use STL in this book. However, the STL implementation of a data structure could be substituted for the student's implementation in most situations where an application program is to be implemented.

Course Planning Guide for the Instructor

The following table is provided to guide you in choosing laboratories and determining sequencing constraints. The recommendations marked as *Required* are laboratories that we consider to contain essential material and, consequently, need to be assigned. If the students do not master the material in those laboratories, they will be at a severe disadvantage when working on later labs. *Suggested* laboratories are those that we recommend assigning as a matter of course. Although we strongly recommend assigning them, they are not essential to successful completion of later labs. *Optional* laboratories are offered for your use based on course emphasis and available time.

Lab Content And Planning Guide

STANDARD LABS

Lab #	Lab Name	Content	Recommendations and Comments
1	Logbook	Classes and abstract data types (ADTs), function and operator overloading.	Recommendation: Suggested Note: Students frequently need to be reacquainted with C++ classes.
2	Point List	Simple list and cursor concept, simple OpenGL graphics application.	Recommendation: Optional
3	List	List operations, dynamic memory allocation, exceptions, Big-O analysis.	Recommendation: Required Note: Future labs depend on the concepts and code introduced in this lab. Suggested reading: Appendix 1, 3
4	Ordered List	Inheritance, sorting based on keys, searching.	Recommendation: Suggested Prerequisite: Lab 3
5	Stack	Templates, postfix expressions, linked implementation with dynamic node allocation, and array-based implementation.	Recommendation: Required Note: Templates and linked structures are used throughout rest of book. Array-based implementation may be skipped if desired. Suggested reading: Appendix 1
6	Queue	Simulation, data structure memory utilization calculation.	Recommendation: Optional
7	Singly-Linked List	Analyze efficiency of linked structures, enhance performance through implementation analysis.	Recommendation: Required
8	Copying and Comparing ADTs	Details of C++ copy and comparison operators.	Recommendation: Required Note: Essential for implementation of complex C++ data structures. Prerequisite: Lab 7
9	Doubly-Linked List	Efficiency comparison with singly-linked list.	Recommendation: Optional
10	Recursion	Recursive problems using linked lists, determining behavior of unexplained recursive functions, conversion of recursive algorithms to iterative form.	Recommendation: Required Note: Lays the foundation for use of recursion in succeeding labs. Prerequisite: Lab 7
11	Binary Search Tree	Introduction to tree structures, application to databases.	Recommendation: Suggested
12	Expression Tree	Use of trees to represent hierarchical data.	Recommendation: Optional
13	Graph	Adjacency matrix representation of graphs, shortest path algorithms.	Recommendation: Optional
14	Hash Table	Hash functions, uniform key distribution, performance analysis.	Recommendation: Optional

ADDITIONAL LABS

Lab #	Lab Name	Content	Recommendations and Comments
A	String	C-strings, overloading operators, copy constructor.	Recommendation: Optional Prerequisite: Lab 1
B	Heap	Heap sort, priority queue, scheduling.	Recommendation: Optional Note: Recommended for advanced students.
C	Performance Evaluation	Performance measurement techniques, searching and sorting algorithms.	Prerequisite: Lab 11 Recommendation: Optional

APPENDIX

1	C++ Program Validation	C++ exceptions and assert statements.	Prerequisite: Labs 4 and 5 Recommendation: Suggested
2	C++ I/O Reference	An explanation of I/O streams and reference listing of member functions.	Note: Exceptions are used throughout the book. Recommendation: Optional
3	C++ Pointers	Pointer usage reference, parameter passing.	Note: Useful for completing lab assignments and projects. Recommendation: Suggested

To the Student

Objectives

The courses that we enjoyed most when we were students were those that emphasized design. In design-oriented courses, we used the concepts taught in lecture to solve practical problems. The process of applying ideas made it easier to understand them and understand how they could be applied in a real-world setting.

This emphasis on learning by doing is used throughout *A Laboratory Course in C++ Data Structures*. In each laboratory, you will explore a particular data structure by implementing it. As you create an implementation, you will learn how the data structure works and how it can be applied. The resulting implementation is a working piece of software that you can use in later laboratories and programming projects.

Organization of the Laboratories

Each laboratory consists of four parts: Prelab, Bridge, In-lab, and Postlab. The **Prelab** is a homework assignment in which you create an implementation of a data structure using the techniques your instructor presents in lecture, along with material from your textbook. In the **Bridge** exercise you test and debug the software you developed in the Prelab. The **In-lab** phase consists of three exercises. In the first exercise, you apply the data structure you created in the Prelab to the solution of a problem. The remaining In-lab exercises apply or extend the concepts introduced in the Prelab. The last part of each laboratory, the **Postlab,** is a homework assignment in which you analyze a data structure in terms of its efficiency or use.

Your instructor will specify which exercises you need to complete for each laboratory. Be sure to check whether your instructor wants you to complete the Bridge exercise prior to your lab period or during lab. Use the cover sheet provided with the laboratory to keep track of the exercises you have been assigned.

Student Resources

The authors have compiled a set of tools that will make it easier for you to create data structure implementations. These tools are available for download at: **http://computerscience.jbpub.com/cppdatastructures/lab_manual.cfm**. For each laboratory, we provide a visualization function that displays a given data structure. You can use this function to watch how your routines change the content and organization of the data structure. Each laboratory also includes an interactive test program that you can use to help you test and debug your work.

Additional files containing data, partial solution shells, and other supporting routines are also available on the lab's web site. You will need these files in order to complete the laboratory exercises.

To the Instructor

Objective

When James Robergé was first given the opportunity to introduce laboratories into his data structures course, he jumped at the chance. He saw laboratories as a way of involving students as active, creative partners in the learning process. By making the laboratories the focal point of the course, he sought to immerse his students in the course material. The goal of each lab is still to challenge students to exercise their creativity (in both programming and analysis) while at the same time providing the structure, feedback, and support that they need to meet the challenge. This manual is the product of years of experimentation and refinement working toward this objective.

Organization of the Laboratories

In the initial development of these labs, it was attempted to shoehorn the creative process into a series of two-hour laboratories. The result was a pressure cooker that challenged everyone, but helped no one. In experimenting with solutions to this problem, James Robergé developed a laboratory framework that retains the creative element but shifts the time-intensive aspects outside the laboratory period. Within this structure, each laboratory includes four parts: Prelab, Bridge, In-lab, and Postlab.

Prelab

The Prelab exercise is a homework assignment that links the lecture with the laboratory period. In the Prelab, students explore and create on their own and at their own pace. Their goal is to synthesize the information they learn in lectures with material from their textbook to produce a working piece of software, usually an implementation of an abstract data type (ADT). A Prelab assignment–including a review of the relevant lecture and textbook materials–typically takes an evening to complete (that is, four to five hours).

Bridge

The Bridge exercise asks students to test the software they developed in the Prelab. The students create a test plan that they then use as a framework for evaluating their code. An interactive, command-driven test program is provided for each laboratory, along with a visualization routine that allows students to see changes in the content and organization of a data structure. This assignment provides an opportunity for students to receive feedback on their Prelab work and to resolve any difficulties they might have encountered. It should take students approximately one hour to finish this exercise.

In-lab

The In-lab section takes place during the actual laboratory period (assuming you are using a closed laboratory setting). Each In-lab consists of three exercises, and each exercise has a distinct role. In Exercise 1, students apply the software they developed in the Prelab to a real-world problem that has been honed to its essentials to fit comfortably within the closed laboratory environment. The last two exercises stress programming, and provide a capstone to the Prelab. Exercise 1 can be completed in approximately one and a half hours. Exercises 2 and 3 take roughly one hour each to complete.

Most students will not be able to complete all the In-lab exercises within a typical closed laboratory period. We have provided a range of exercises so that you can select those that best suit your laboratory environment and your students' needs.

Postlab

The last phase of each laboratory is a homework assignment to be done following the laboratory period. In the Postlab, students analyze the efficiency or utility of a given data structure. Each Postlab exercise should take roughly thirty minutes to complete.

Using the Four-Part Organization in Your Laboratory Environment

The term *laboratory* is used by computer science instructors to denote a broad range of environments. One group of students in a data structures course, for example, may attend a closed two-hour laboratory; at the same time, another group of students may take the class in a televised format and "attend" an open laboratory. In developing this manual, we have preserved the first edition's efforts to create a laboratory format suitable for a variety of open and closed laboratory settings. How you use the four-part organization depends on your laboratory environment.

Two-Hour Closed Laboratory

Prelab

We expect the students attending a two-hour closed laboratory to make a good-faith effort to complete the Prelab exercise before coming to the lab. Their work need not be perfect, but their effort must be real (roughly 80% correct).

Bridge

We ask our students to complete the test plans included in the Bridge exercise and to begin testing and debugging their Prelab work prior to coming to lab (as part of the 80% correct guideline).

In-lab

We use the first hour of the laboratory period to resolve any problems the students might have experienced in completing the Prelab and Bridge exercises. Our intention is to give constructive feedback so that students leave the lab with working Prelab software—a significant accomplishment on their part.

During the second hour, we have students complete one of the In-lab exercises to reinforce the concepts learned in the Prelab. You can choose the exercise by section or by student, or you can let the students decide which one to complete.

Students leave the lab having received feedback on their Prelab and In-lab work. You need not rigidly enforce the hourly divisions; a mix of activities keeps everyone interested and motivated.

Postlab

After the lab, the students complete one of the Postlab exercises and turn it in during their next lab period.

One-Hour Closed Laboratory

Prelab

If we have only one hour for the closed laboratory, we ask students to complete both the Prelab and Bridge exercises before they come to the lab. This work is turned in at the start of the period.

In-lab
During the laboratory period, the students complete one of the In-lab exercises.

Postlab
Again, the students complete one of the Postlab exercises and submit it during their next lab period.

Open Laboratory

In an open laboratory setting, we have the students complete the Prelab and Bridge exercises, one of the In-lab exercises, and one of the Postlab exercises. You can stagger the submission of these exercises throughout the week or have students turn in the entire laboratory as a unit.

Adapting the Manual to Your Course

Student Preparation

This manual assumes that students have a background in either C or C++. The first laboratory introduces classes and the use of classes to implement a simple ADT. Succeeding laboratories introduce more complex C++ language features (dynamic memory allocation, templates, inheritance, and so forth) in the context of data structures that use these features.

Order of Topics

All instructors cover the course material in the order that they believe best suits their students' needs. To give instructors flexibility in the order of presentation, we have made the individual laboratories as independent of one another as possible. We recommend beginning with the following sequence of laboratories.

Laboratory 1 (*Logbook ADT*)
    Introduces the implementation of an ADT using C++ classes

Laboratory 3 (*Array Implementation of the List ADT*)
    Introduces dynamic memory allocation

Laboratory 5 (Stack ADT)
    Introduces linked lists

We have placed the performance evaluation laboratory at the end of the manual (Laboratory C), because in our experience, we have found that everyone covers this topic at a different time. Rather than bury it in the middle of the manual, we have placed it at the end so that you can include it where it best serves your and your students' needs, be that early in the semester, in the middle, or toward the end.

ADT Implementation

The laboratories are designed to complement a variety of approaches to implementing each ADT. All ADT definitions stress the use of data abstraction and generic data elements. As a result, you can adapt them with minimal effort to suit different implementation strategies.

For each ADT, class declarations that frame an implementation of the ADT are given as part of the corresponding Prelab exercise. This declaration framework is also used in the visualization function that accompanies the laboratory. Should you elect to adopt a somewhat different implementation strategy, you need only make minor changes to the data members in the class declarations and corresponding modifications to the visualization routine. You do not need to change anything else in either the supplied software or the laboratory text itself.

Differences Between the Manual and Your Text

We have found that variations in style between the approaches used in the textbook and the laboratory manual discourage students from simply copying material from the textbook. Having to make changes, however slight, encourages them to examine in more detail how a given implementation works.

Combining the Laboratories with Programming Projects

One of our goals in designing these laboratories was to enable students to produce in the laboratory code that they can use again as part of larger, more applications-oriented programming projects. The ADTs the students develop in the Prelab exercises provide a solid foundation for such projects. Reusing the material that they created in laboratory frees students to focus on the application they are developing. More important, they see in concrete terms - their time and effort - the value of such essential software engineering concepts as code reuse, data abstraction, and object-oriented programming.

The first exercise in each In-lab is an applications problem based on the material covered in the Prelab for that laboratory. These exercises provide an excellent starting point for programming projects. Free-form projects are also possible.

Student Resources

Challenging students is easy; helping them to meet a challenge is not. The student resources found on **http://computerscience.jbpub.com/cppdatastructures/ lab_manual.cfm** include a set of software tools that assist students in developing ADT implementations. The tools provide students with the means for testing an ADT implementation using simple keyboard commands and for visualizing the resulting data structure using ASCII text on a standard text display. Additional files containing data, partial solution shells, and other supporting routines are also available for download.

Instructor's Resources

An Instructor's Solutions Kit is available for download at **http://computerscience. jbpub.com/cppdatastructures/lab_manual.cfm**. Solutions to all of the Prelab and In-lab exercises are included. Instructors should contact their Jones and Bartlett Publishers Representative at 1-800-832-0034 for the password, in order to access the Instructor's Kit.

Acknowledgments

Writing this type of lab manual is an "iceberg" project—much of the work goes into the implementation of a programming infrastructure that is only somewhat visible on the printed page. We would like to thank Michael Stranz and Amy Rose for their patience in guiding this particular iceberg through the publication process. We would like to thank the following reviewers of the first edition's manuscript: John W. Fendrich of Bradley University, Timothy R. Hines of Johnson County Community College, Reggie Kwan of Montana Tech, and Keith B. Olson of the University of Montana. Thanks also to George Smith, Sunil Nair, Inhee Song, and Beomjin Kim for their comments on earlier drafts of these laboratories.

I especially wish to thank Bob Carlson and Charlie Bauer for providing the leadership that made a laboratory-based curriculum a priority in our department. Their advice and encouragement means a great deal to me. Finally, I owe an unpayable debt of thanks to my wife Ruby for her patience and support amid all the chaos.

J.R.

We would like to thank James Robergé for the vision and hard work that resulted in the first edition, Jones and Bartlett Publishers for their faith and patience, Beth Holloway for help with many of the details of this project, the Taylor University Computing and System Sciences Department for their support, and our families and friends for their encouragement and understanding.

S.B. & D.W.

contents

Logbook ADT

In this laboratory you will:

■ Examine the components that form an abstract data type (ADT)

■ Implement an ADT using a C++ class

■ Create a function that displays a logbook in calendar form

■ Investigate how to overload functions and operators

Objectives

Overview

The purpose of this laboratory is for you to explore how you can use C++ classes to implement an abstract data type (ADT). We use a monthly logbook as our example abstract data type. A **monthly logbook** consists of a set of entries, one for each day of the month. Depending on the logbook, these entries might denote a business's daily receipts, the amount of time a person spent exercising, the number of cups of coffee consumed, and so forth. A typical logbook is shown below.

February 2003															
														1	100
2	95	3	90	4	0	5	150	6	94	7	100	8	105		
9	100	10	100	11	50	12	110	13	110	14	100	15	125		
16	110	17	0	18	110	19	0	20	125	21	100	22	110		
23	115	24	111	25	0	26	50	27	110	28	125				

C++ provides a set of predefined data types (int, char, float, and so on). Each of these predefined types has a set of operations associated with it. You use these operations to manipulate variables of a given type. For example, type int supports the basic arithmetic and relational operators, as well as a number of numerical functions (abs(), div(), etc.). These predefined data types provide a foundation on which you construct more sophisticated data types, data types that are collections of related data items rather than individual data items. In order to distinguish the data types you create from C++'s predefined data types, we refer to them as **abstract data types** or ADTs.

When specifying an ADT, you begin by describing what type of data items are in the ADT. Then you describe how the ADT data items are organized to form the ADT's **structure**. In the case of the monthly logbook abstract data type—or Logbook ADT, for short—the data items are the entries associated with the days of the month and the structure is linear: the entries are arranged in the same order as the corresponding days.

Having specified the data items and the structure of the ADT, you then define how the ADT can be used by specifying the **operations** that are associated with the ADT. For each operation, you specify what conditions must be true before the operation can be applied (its preconditions or **requirements**) as well as what conditions will be true after the operation has completed (its postconditions or **results**). The following Logbook ADT specification includes operations that create a logbook for a given month, store/retrieve the logbook entry for a specific day, and provide general information about the month.

Logbook ADT

Data Items

A set of integer values.

Structure

Each integer value is the logbook entry for a given day of the month. The number of logbook entries varies depending on the month for which data is being recorded. We will refer to this month as the **logbook month**.

Operations

```
Logbook ( int month, int year )
```

Requirements:
Month must specify a valid month.

Results:
Constructor. Creates an empty logbook for the specified month—that is, a logbook in which all the entries are zero.

```
void putEntry ( int day, int value )
```

Requirements:
Day is within the range of days in the logbook month.

Results:
Stores the value as the logbook entry for the specified day.

```
int getEntry ( int day )
```

Requirements:
Day is within the range of days in the logbook month.

Results:
Returns the logbook entry for the specified day.

```
int getMonth () const
```

Requirements:
None

Results:
Returns the logbook month.

```
int getYear () const
```

Requirements:
None

Results:
Returns the logbook year.


```
int getDaysInMonth () const
```

Requirements:
None

Results:
Returns the number of days in the logbook month.

Laboratory 1: Cover Sheet

Name _____ Date _____

Section _____

Place a check mark in the *Assigned* column next to the exercises your instructor has assigned to you. Attach this cover sheet to the front of the packet of materials you submit following the laboratory.

Activities	Assigned: Check or list exercise numbers	Completed
Prelab Exercise		
Bridge Exercise		
In-lab Exercise 1		
In-lab Exercise 2		
In-lab Exercise 3		
Postlab Exercise 1		
Postlab Exercise 2		
Total		

Laboratory 1: Prelab Exercise

Name _____ Date _____

Section _____

The Logbook ADT specification provides enough information for you (or other programmers) to design and develop programs that use logbooks. Before you can begin using logbooks in your C++ programs, however, you must first create a C++ implementation of the Logbook ADT.

You saw in the Overview that an ADT consists of a set of data items and a set of operations that manipulate these data items. A C++ **class** consists of a set of **data members** and a set of **member functions** that manipulate these data members. This close relationship between ADTs and classes makes classes a natural means for implementing ADTs.

How do you create a declaration for a Logbook class from the specification of the Logbook ADT? You begin with the ADT data items and structure. The Logbook ADT specification indicates that you must maintain the following information about each logbook:

- The (month,year) pair that specifies the logbook month
- The logbook entries for the month

This information is stored in the data members of the Logbook class. The month and year are stored as integer values and the entries are stored as an array of integers.

```
class Logbook
  {
    ...

    private:

      // Data members
      int logMonth,      // Month covered by logbook
          logYear,       // Year for this logbook
          entries[31];   // Logbook entries
  };
```

By declaring the data members to be **private**, you prevent nonmember functions—that is, functions that are not members of the Logbook class—from accessing the logbook data directly. This restriction ensures that all references to the logbook data are made using the operations in the Logbook ADT.

Having specified how the logbook data is to be stored, you then add declarations for the member functions corresponding to the operations in the Logbook ADT. These functions are declared as **public**. They can be called by any function, either member or nonmember, and provide a **public interface** to the logbook data.

```
class Logbook
{
  public:

    // Constructor
    Logbook ( int month, int year );          // Create a logbook
```

```
    // Logbook marking operations
    void putEntry ( int day, int value );      // Store entry for day
    int getEntry ( int day ) const;            // Return entry for day

    // General operations
    int getMonth () const;                     // Return the month
    int getYear () const;                      // Return the year
    int getDaysInMonth () const;               // Number of days in month

  private:

    ...
    // Data members
    int logMonth,         // Month covered by logbook
        logYear,          // Year for this logbook
        entries[31];      // Logbook entries
};
```

You need to know whether a given year is a leap year in order to determine the number of days in a month. Adding a **facilitator function** (or helper function) that determines this information completes the declaration of the Logbook class. Note that the facilitator function is *not* an operation in the Logbook ADT. Thus, it is included as a private member function rather than as part of the public interface. The completed Logbook class declaration follows. This declaration is stored in the header file *logbook.h.*

```
class Logbook
{
  public:

    // Constructor
    Logbook ( int month, int year );          // Create a logbook

    // Logbook marking operations
    void putEntry ( int day, int value );      // Store entry for day
    int getEntry ( int day ) const;            // Return entry for day

    // General operations
    int getMonth () const;                     // Return the month
    int getYear () const;                      // Return the year
    int getDaysInMonth () const;               // Number of days in month

  private:

    // Facilitator (helper) function
    bool isLeapYear () const;                  // Leap year?

    // Data members
    int logMonth,         // Month covered by logbook
        logYear,          // Year for this logbook
        entries[31];      // Logbook entries
};
```

The Logbook class declaration provides a framework for the Logbook class. You fill in this framework by implementing each of the member functions. An implementation of the `getMonth()` function is given below.

```cpp
int Logbook:: getMonth () const
// Returns the logbook month.
{
    return logMonth;
}
```

Note the use of the scope resolution operator (::) to indicate that `getMonth()` is a member function in the Logbook class. You store your implementation of the member functions in the file *logbook.cpp*.

The class declaration in the file *logbook.h* and the code in the file *logbook.cpp* form a C++ implementation of the Logbook ADT. The following application program uses the Logbook ADT to record and output a set of logbook entries. Note that this program would ordinarily be stored in its own file (called *coffee.cpp*, for instance).

```cpp
#include <iostream>
#include "logbook.h"    // Include the declaration of the Logbook class

using namespace std;

// Records coffee intake for January 2003.

void main ()
{
    Logbook coffee(1,2003);    // Coffee intake for January 2003
    int day;                   // Day loop counter

    // Record entries for the 1st and 15th of January 2003

    coffee.putEntry(1,5);
    coffee.putEntry(15,2);

    // Output the logbook entries.

    cout << "Month/Year : " << coffee.getMonth() << "/"
         << coffee.getYear() << endl;

    for ( day = 1 ; day <= coffee.getDaysInMonth() ; day++ )
        cout << day << " : " << coffee.getEntry(day) << endl;
}
```

The declaration

```cpp
Logbook coffee(1,2003);
```

invokes the Logbook class constructor to create a logbook for January 2003. The constructor begins by setting `logMonth` to 1 and `logYear` to 2003. You can use the assignment operator to perform this task, as in the following code fragment.

```
Logbook::Logbook ( int month, int year )
// Constructs an empty logbook for the specified month.
{
    logMonth = month;
    logYear  = year;
    ...                     // Set each entry in the logbook to 0.
}
```

Or, you can use a member initialization list to initialize `logMonth` and `logYear`. The syntax for a member initialization list is shown below. Note that there is no semicolon at the end of the initialization list.

```
Logbook::Logbook ( int month, int year )
// Constructs an empty logbook for the specified month.
  : logMonth(month),
    logYear(year)
{
    ...                     // Set each entry in the logbook to 0.
}
```

These two methods of performing the initialization are roughly equivalent, so the choice is generally a matter of preference. However, there are cases in C++ where initialization can only be performed using the member initialization list.

Once the constructor has assigned values to `logMonth` and `logYear`, it sets each data item in the `entries` array to 0 and returns.

Having constructed an empty logbook, the program then uses the `putEntry()` function to record a pair of logbook entries. It then outputs the logbook using repeated calls to the `getEntry()` function, with the `getMonth()` and `getYear()` functions providing output headings.

A significant implementation issue is what to do when a logbook function such as `putEntry()` or `getEntry()` is called with parameters that do not meet the stated requirements. Using the `getEntry()` function as an example, it is a logic error to request the entry for an invalid day. Although there are many possible ways of dealing with this situation, the standard C++ method for dealing with bad parameters and other difficult—or impossible—situations is to **throw** an **exception**.

You will start using C++ exceptions in lab 3, the List ADT. Until then, implement all class member functions as though the requirements (preconditions) for each function have been met. That is, you may assume that all function parameters are valid and that the functions will not be asked to do anything illogical.

Step 1: Implement the member functions in the Logbook class. Base your implementation on the Logbook class declaration given above (and in the file *logbook.h*).

Step 2: Save your implementation of the Logbook ADT in the file *logbook.cpp*. Be sure to document your code.

Laboratory 1: Bridge Exercise

Name _____ Date _____

Section _____

Check with your instructor whether you are to complete this exercise prior to your lab period or during lab.

Test your implementation of the Logbook ADT using the program in the file *test1.cpp*. This program supports the following tests.

Test	Action
1	Tests the constructor and the `getMonth`, `getYear`, and `getDaysInMonth` operations.
2	Tests the `putEntry` and `getEntry` operations.

Step 1: Compile your implementation of the Logbook ADT in the file *logbook.cpp*.

Step 2: Compile the test program in the file *test1.cpp*.

Step 3: Link the object files produced by Steps 1 and 2.

Step 4: Complete the test plan for Test 1 by filling in the expected number of days for each month.

Step 5: Execute the test plan. If you discover mistakes in your implementation of the Logbook ADT, correct them and execute the test plan again.

Test Plan for Test 1 (`constructor`, `month`, `year`, and `daysInMonth` operations)

Test Case	Logbook Month	# Days in Month	Checked
Simple month	1 2003	31	
Month in the past	7 1969		
Month in the future	12 2011		
Current month			
February (nonleap year)	2 2003		
February (leap year)	2 2004		

Step 6: Complete the test plan for Test 2 by filling in the input data and expected result for each test case. Use a logbook for the current month.

Step 7: Execute the test plan. If you discover mistakes in your implementation of the Logbook ADT, correct them and execute the test plan again.

Test Plan for Test 2 (putEntry and getEntry operations)

Test Case	Logbook Entries	Expected Result	Checked
Record entries for the first and fifteenth of the month	1 100 15 200		
Record entries for the first and last day of the month			
Record entries for all the Fridays in the month			
Record an entry for the first day twice	1 100 1 300		

Laboratory 1: In-lab Exercise 1

Name _____ Date _____

Section _____

The entries in a logbook store information about a specific month. A calendar provides a natural format for displaying this monthly data.

```
void displayCalendar () const
```

Requirements:
Logbook month must occur in a year in the range 1901–2099.

Results:
Outputs a logbook using the calendar format shown below. Note that each calendar entry includes the logbook entry for the corresponding day.

```
                        2 / 2003
    Sun       Mon       Tue      Wed       Thu       Fri       Sat
                                                            1 100
  2 95      3 90      4 0       5 150    6 94      7 100     8 105
  9 100    10 100    11 50     12 110   13 110    14 100    15 125
 16 110    17 0      18 110    19 0     20 125    21 100    22 110
 23 115    24 111    25 0      26 50    27 110    28 125
```

In order to produce a calendar for a given month, you need to know on which day of the week the first day of the month occurs. The day of the week corresponding to a date *month/day/year* can be computed using the following formula:

$$dayOfWeek = (1 + nYears + nLeapYears + nDaysToMonth + day) \% 7$$

where *nYears* is the number of years since 1901, *nLeapYears* is the number of leap years since 1901, and *nDaysToMonth* is the number of days from the start of the year to the start of *month*. This formula yields a value between 0 (Sunday) and 6 (Saturday) and is accurate for any date from January 1, 1901 to December 31, 2099. You can compute the value *nDaysToMonth* dynamically using a loop. Alternatively, you can use an array to store the number of days before each month in a nonleap year and add a correction for leap years when needed.

Step 1: Implement the facilitator function `getDayOfWeek()` described below and add it to the file *logbook.cpp*. A prototype for this function is included in the declaration of the Logbook class in the file *logbook.h*.

```
int getDayOfWeek ( int day ) const
```

Requirements:

Day is a valid day in the logbook month (must occur during a year in the range 1901–2099).

Results:

Returns an integer denoting the day of the week on which the specified day occurs, where 0 corresponds to Sunday, 1 to Monday, and so forth.

Step 2: Implement the `displayCalendar` operation described above and add it to the file *logbook.cpp*. A prototype for this operation is included in the declaration of the Logbook class in the file *logbook.h*.

Step 3: Activate Test 3 in the test program *test1.cpp* by removing the comment delimiter (and the character '3') from the lines that begin with "//3".

Step 4: Complete the test plan for Test 3 by filling in the day of the week for the first day of the current month.

Step 5: Execute the test plan. If you discover mistakes in your implementation of the `displayCalendar` operation, correct them and execute the test plan again.

Test Plan for Test 3 (`displayCalendar` operation)

Test Case	Logbook Month	Day of the Week of the First Day in the Month	Checked
Simple month	1 1995	0 (Sunday)	
Month in the past	7 1969	2 (Tuesday)	
Month in the future	12 2011	4 (Thursday)	
Current month			
February (nonleap year)	2 2003	6 (Saturday)	
February (leap year)	2 2004	0 (Sunday)	

Laboratory 1: In-lab Exercise 2

Name _____ Date _____

Section _____

C++ allows you to create multiple functions with the same name as long as these functions have different numbers of arguments or different types of arguments—a process referred to as **function overloading**. The following Logbook ADT operations, for example, each share the same name as an existing operation. They have fewer arguments than the existing operations, however. Instead of using an argument to specify the month (or day) to process, they use the current month (or day).

```
Logbook ()
```
Requirements:
None

Results:
Default constructor. Creates an empty logbook for the current month.

```
void putEntry ( int value )
```
Requirements:
Logbook is for the current month.

Results:
Stores the value as the logbook entry for today.

Step 1: Implement these operations and add them to the file *logbook.cpp*. Prototypes for these operations are included in the declaration of the Logbook class in the file *logbook.h*. The standard C++ library functions time() and localtime() can be used to access the necessary time and date information. You may need help from your instructor to get this working.

Step 2: Activate Test 4 in the test program *test1.cpp* by removing the comment delimiter (and the character '4') from the lines that begin with "//4".

Step 3: Complete the test plan for Test 4 by filling in the expected result for each operation.

Step 4: Execute the test plan. If you discover mistakes in your implementation of these operations, correct them and execute the test plan again.

Test Plan for Test 4 (overloaded functions)

Test Case	Expected Result	Checked
Construct a logbook for the current month	Number of days in the current month:	
Record an entry for today	Day on which entry is made:	

Laboratory 1: In-lab Exercise 3

Name _____   Date _____

Section _____

C++ allows you to create operators that share the name of one of C++'s predefined operators, a process referred to as **operator overloading**. The following operation, for instance, uses the syntax of the familiar subscript operator to retrieve logbook entries. It is functionally equivalent to the getEntry operation.

```
int operator [] ( int day ) const
```

Requirements:
Day is within the valid range of days in the logbook month.

Results:
Returns the logbook entry for the specified day.

The following operation provides another example of operator overloading. In this case, the additive assignment operator (+=) is used to combine logbooks.

```
void operator += ( const Logbook &rightLogbook )
```

Requirements:
The logbooks cover the same month.

Results:
Adds each entry in rightLogBook to the corresponding entry in this logbook.

The following code fragment uses these operations to sum a pair of logbooks and output the combined logbook entries.

```
Logbook citySales(9,2003),      // City sales
        suburbSales(9,2003),    // Suburban sales
        salesTotals(9,2003);    // Combined sales for September 2003
int j;                          // Loop counter

// Read in the city and suburban sales.
...

// Sum the city and suburban sales.

salesTotals += citySales;       // Include city sales
salesTotals += suburbSales;     // Include suburban sales

// Output the sum.

for ( j = 1 ; j <= salesTotals.getDaysInMonth() ; j++ )
    cout << j << " : " << salesTotals[j] << endl;
```

Step 1: Implement these operations and add them to the file *logbook.cpp*. Prototypes for these operations are included in the declaration of the Logbook class in the file *logbook.h*.

Step 2: Activate Test 5 in the test program *test1.cpp* by removing the comment delimiter (and the character '5') from the lines that begin with "//5".

Step 3: Complete the test plan for Test 5 by filling in the input data and expected result for each test case. Use a logbook for the current month.

Step 4: Execute the test plan. If you discover mistakes in your implementation of the subscript operation, correct them and execute the test plan again.

Test Plan for Test 5 ([ ] operation)

Test Case	Logbook Entries	Expected Result	Checked
Record entries for the first and fifteenth of the month	2 100 15 200		
Record entries for the first and last day of the month			

Step 5: Activate Test 6 in the test program *test1.cpp* by removing the comment delimiter (and the character '6') from the lines that begin with "//6".

Step 6: Complete the test plan for Test 6 by filling in the expected result. Use a logbook for the current month.

Step 7: Execute the test plan. If you discover mistakes in your implementation of the logbook addition operation, correct them and execute the test plan again.

Test Plan for Test 6 (+= operation)

Test Case	Expected Result of Adding `logDay200` to `logDay100`	Checked
The entries in logbook `logDay100` are equal to (100 * day) and the entries in logbook `logDay200` are equal to (200 * day)		

Laboratory 1: Postlab Exercise 1

Name _____   Date _____

Section _____

Part A

The following function prototypes are part of the declaration of the Logbook class.

```
int getMonth () const;        // Return the month
int getYear () const;         // Return the year
int getDaysInMonth () const;  // Number of days in month
```

What is the significance of the keyword `const` in these prototypes?

Part B

Why are some member functions `const` and others not?

Laboratory 1: Postlab Exercise 2

Name _____   Date _____

Section _____

Part A

What is the significance of the keyword `const` and the symbol '&' in the following function prototype from In-lab Exercise 3?

```
void operator += ( const Logbook &rightLogbook )
```

Part B

What is gained by passing `rightLogbook` in this way?

Point List ADT

In this laboratory you will:

- Implement a list of points using an array representation of a list, including development of an iteration scheme that allows you to move through a list data item by data item

- Become familiar with the concept of using a cursor to focus on a particular item in a data structure

- Create a program—using OpenGL—that displays a curve represented as a point list

- Develop a function to determine whether one point list represents a translation of another point list

Overview

The list is perhaps the most commonly used data structure. Just think how often you make lists of things to do, places to be, and so on. The defining property of a **list** is that the data items are organized linearly—that is, every data item has one data item immediately before it and another immediately after it (except, of course, the data items at the beginning and end of the list).

In this laboratory, you explore lists in which each data item is a two-dimensional point, or (x, y) pair. We refer to this type of list as a **point list**. Point lists are routinely used in computer graphics, computer-aided design (CAD), and computer modeling to represent lines, curves, edges, and so forth.

The following Point List ADT provides operations that allow you to add points to a list, check the state of a list (is it empty or is it full?), and iterate through the points in a list. **List iteration** is the process of moving through a list, processing each data item in turn. Iteration is done using a **cursor** that you move through the list much as you move the cursor in a text editor or word processor. In the following example, the Point List ADT's gotoBeginning operation is used to move the cursor to the beginning of the list. The cursor is then moved through the list point-by-point by repeated applications of the gotoNext operation. Note that the point marked by the cursor is shown in bold.

After gotoBeginning: **(0,0)** (1,1) (2,2) (3,3)

After gotoNext: (0,0) **(1,1)** (2,2) (3,3)

After gotoNext: (0,0) (1,1) **(2,2)** (3,3)

After gotoNext: (0,0) (1,1) (2,2) **(3,3)**

Point List ADT

Data Items

Each data item in a point list is of type Point and contains a pair of floating-point numbers that represent the point's x and y coordinates.

Structure

The points form a linear structure in which points follow one after the other, from the beginning of the list to its end. The ordering of the points is determined by the order in which they were appended to the list. At any point in time, one point in any nonempty list is marked using the list's cursor. You travel through the list using operations that change the position of the cursor.

Operations

```
PointList ()
```

Requirements:
None

Results:
Constructor. Creates an empty list.

```
void append ( Point newPoint )
```

Requirements:
List is not full.

Results:
Adds newPoint to the end of a list. If the list is empty, then adds newPoint as the first (and only) point in the list. In either case, moves the cursor to newPoint.

```
void clear ()
```

Requirements:
None

Results:
Removes all the points in a list.

```
bool isEmpty () const
```

Requirements:
None

Results:
Returns `true` if a list is empty. Otherwise, returns `false`.

```
bool isFull () const
```

Requirements:
None

Results:
Returns `true` if a list is full. Otherwise, returns `false`.

```
void gotoBeginning ()
```

Requirements:
List is not empty.

Results:
Moves the cursor to the point at the beginning of the list.

```
void gotoEnd ()
```

Requirements:
List is not empty.

Results:
Moves the cursor to the point at the end of the list.

```
bool gotoNext ()
```

Requirements:
List is not empty.

Results:
If the cursor is not at the end of a list, then moves the cursor to the next point in the list and returns `true`. Otherwise, returns `false`.

```
bool gotoPrior ()
```

Requirements:
List is not empty.

Results:
If the cursor is not at the beginning of a list, then moves the cursor to the preceding point in the list and returns `true`. Otherwise, returns `false`.

```
Point getCursor () const
```

Requirements:
List is not empty.

Results:
Returns a copy of the point marked by the cursor.

```
void showStructure () const
```

Requirements:
None

Results:
Outputs the points in a list. If the list is empty, outputs "Empty list". Note that this operation is intended for testing/debugging purposes only.

Laboratory 2: Cover Sheet

Name _____ Date _____

Section _____

Place a check mark in the *Assigned* column next to the exercises your instructor has assigned to you. Attach this cover sheet to the front of the packet of materials you submit following the laboratory.

Activities	Assigned: Check or list exercise numbers	Completed
Prelab Exercise		
Bridge Exercise		
In-lab Exercise 1		
In-lab Exercise 2		
In-lab Exercise 3		
Postlab Exercise 1		
Postlab Exercise 2		
Total		

Laboratory 2: Prelab Exercise

Name _____ Date _____

Section _____

You can implement a list in many ways. Given that a list is linear and that all the list data items are of the same type (Point), an array seems a natural choice. It would be more flexible if you could declare the size of the array at run-time (this will happen in Lab 3, the list ADT), but for now the array size will be fixed.

Step 1: Implement the operations in the Point List ADT using an array to store the list of points. The number of data items in a list changes, therefore you need to store the actual number of points in the list (size), along with the points themselves (points). You also need to keep track of the array index (cursor). Base your implementation on the following declarations from the file *ptlist.h*. An implementation of the showStructure operation is given in the file *show2.cpp*.

```
const int maxListSize = 10;      // Default maximum list size

class Point
{
  public:

    Point ( float x0 = 0, float y0 = 0 )    // Constructor
      { x = x0; y = y0; }

    float x, y;    // Point coordinates (can be accessed directly)
};

class PointList
{
  public:

    // Constructor
    PointList ();

    // List manipulation operations
    void append ( Point newPoint );    // Append point to list
    void clear ();                     // Clear list

    // List status operations
    bool isEmpty () const;             // List is empty
    bool isFull () const;              // List is full

    // List iteration operations
    void gotoBeginning ();             // Go to beginning
    void gotoEnd ();                   // Go to end
    bool gotoNext ();                  // Go to next point
    bool gotoPrior ();                 // Go to prior point
    Point getCursor () const;          // Return point
```

```
     // Output the list structure — used in testing/debugging
     void showStructure () const;

  private:

     // Data members
     int size,                    // Actual number of points in the list
         cursor;                  // Cursor index
     Point points[maxListSize];   // Array containing the points
};
```

Step 2: Save your implementation of the Point List ADT in the file *ptlist.cpp*. Be sure to document your code.

The declarations in the file *ptlist.h* and the code in the file *ptlist.cpp* combine to form a C++ implementation of the Point List ADT. The following code fragment uses the operations in this ADT to construct a list of points and to iterate through the list from beginning to end, outputting each point along the way.

```
#include <iostream>
#include "ptlist.h"

using namespace std;

void main ()
{
    PointList polygon;    // Set of vertices for a polygon
    Point vertex;         // Vertex

    // Read in the polygon's vertices.

    cout << "Enter the polygon's vertices (end with eof) : ";
    while ( cin >> vertex.x >> vertex.y && !polygon.isFull() )
        polygon.append(vertex);

    // Output the vertices one per line.

    if ( !polygon.isEmpty() )
    {
       polygon.gotoBeginning();              // Go to beginning of list
       do
       {
          vertex = polygon.getCursor();
          cout << "(" << vertex.x << ","
               << vertex.y << ")" << endl;
       }
       while ( polygon.gotoNext() );        // Go to next point (if any)
    }
}
```

Laboratory 2: Bridge Exercise

Name _____   Date _____

Section _____

Check with your instructor whether you are to complete this exercise prior to your lab period or during lab.

The test program you used in Laboratory 1 consisted of a series of tests that were hardcoded into the program. Adding a new test case to this style of test program requires changing the test program itself. In this laboratory, you use a more flexible kind of test program to evaluate your ADT implementation—one in which you specify a test case using commands, rather than code. This interactive, command-driven test program allows you to check a new test case by simply entering a series of keyboard commands and observing the results.

The test program in the file *test2.cpp* supports the following commands.

Command	Action
+ x y	Append point (x,y) to the end of the list.
@	Display the point marked by the cursor.
N	Go to the next point.
P	Go to the prior point.
<	Go to the beginning of the list.
>	Go to the end of the list.
E	Report whether the list is empty.
F	Report whether the list is full.
C	Clear the list.
Q	Quit the test program.

Suppose you wish to confirm that your array implementation of the Point List ADT successfully constructs a point list storing the vertices of a square. You can test this case by entering the following sequence of keyboard commands.

Command	+ 1 1	+ 1 2	+ 2 2	+ 2 1	Q
Action	Append (1,1)	Append (1,2)	Append (2,2)	Append (2,1)	Quit

It is easy to see how this interactive test program allows you to rapidly examine a variety of test cases. This speed comes with a price, however. You must be careful not to violate the preconditions required by the operations you are testing. For instance, the commands

Command	C	@
Action	Clear list	Error

cause the test program to fail during the call to the getCursor operation. The source of the failure does not lie in the implementation of the Point List ADT, nor is the test program flawed. The failure occurs because this sequence of operations creates a state that violates the preconditions of the `getCursor` operation (the list must *not* be empty when the getCursor operation is invoked). The speed with which you can create and evaluate test cases using an interactive, command-driven test program makes it very easy to produce this kind of error. It is very tempting to just sit down and start entering commands. A much better strategy, however, is to create a test plan listing the test cases you wish to check and then to write out command sequences that generate these test cases.

Step 1: Compile your implementation of the Point List ADT in the file *ptlist.cpp*, the test program in the file *test2.cpp*, and link them together into one executable.

Step 2: Complete the following test plan by adding test cases that check whether your implementation of the Point List ADT correctly handles the following tasks:

- Appending points to a list that has been cleared
- Filling a list to its maximum size
- Determining whether a list is empty
- Determining whether a list is full

Assume that the output of one test case is used as the input to the following test case and note that although expected results are listed for the final command in each command sequence, you should confirm that *each* command produces a correct result.

Step 3: Execute your test plan. If you discover mistakes in your implementation of the Point List ADT, correct them and execute your test plan again.

Test Plan for the Operations in the Point List ADT

Test Case	Commands	Expected Result	Checked
Append a series of points	+ 1 2 + 3 4 + 5 6 + 7 8	(1,2) (3,4) (5,6) (7,8)	
Iterate from the beginning	< N N	(1,2) (3,4) (5,6) (7,8)	
Iterate from the end	> P P	(1,2) (3,4) (5,6) (7,8)	
Display the point marked by the cursor	@	(3,4)	
Clear the list	C	Empty list	

Note: The point marked by the cursor is shown in **bold**.

Laboratory 2: In-lab Exercise 1

Name _____   Date _____

Section _____

As we noted in the Overview, point lists are commonly used in computer graphics to represent curves. Rather than storing all the points required to display a curve at a given level of detail—an approach that would require massive amounts of storage—only selected points are stored in the list. These points are then connected by line segments when the curve is displayed (through the "connect the dots" game). The figure below shows a circle centered at (2,2) with radius 1, its point list representation, and the resulting display.

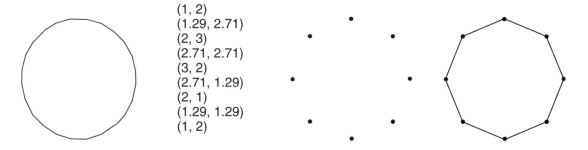

(1, 2)
(1.29, 2.71)
(2, 3)
(2.71, 2.71)
(3, 2)
(2.71, 1.29)
(2, 1)
(1.29, 1.29)
(1, 2)

Note that we have sacrificed some of the smoothness of the circle by approximating it using only nine points (with one point repeated so that the curve is closed). We could produce a much smoother circle by dividing the circle into smaller pieces.

Step 1:   Using the shell in the file *drawcurv.cs* as a basis, create a program that displays the points in a point list. Your program need only display the points themselves, *not* the lines connecting them.

Step 2:   Test your program using a square. Call the `makeSquare()` function (in the file *drawcurv.cs*) to generate the point list for a square.

Step 3:   Test your program using a dragon curve. Call the `makeDragon()` function (in the file *drawcurv.cs*) to generate the point list for a dragon curve. The point lists for dragon curves grow quite large as the recursion depth is increased. *Note:* This will require you to change the `maxListSize` in *ptlist.h* to make the array big enough to hold enough points.

Step 4:   Modify your program so that it displays the line segment connecting each pair of points in a point list.

Step 5:   Test your modified program using a square and a dragon curve.

Test Plan for the Curve Drawing Program

Test Case	Expected Curve	Checked
Square		
Dragon curve (recursion depth 2)		
Dragon curve (recursion depth 7)		

Laboratory 2: In-lab Exercise 2

Name _____   Date _____

Section _____

```
bool isTranslation ( const PointList &otherList )
```

Requirements:
None

Results:
Compares the contents of the current PointList object to otherList in order to determine whether otherList represents a translation of the current PointList object. Returns `true` if it represents a translation. Otherwise, returns `false`. If the lists are not the same size or are empty, then they do not represent a translation.

In the field of computer graphics, it is common to take a set of points and make one or more changes to all the points to produce a new set of points. Scaling enables the zoom effect. Rotation is used to achieve—surprise—rotation of images. Translation moves a set of points without performing a rotation. To translate a single two-dimensional point (x, y), the x value can be changed by a specific amount—called delta-x (Δx)—and the y value can be changed by another amount, delta-y (Δy). To translate a set of points, the same Δx and Δy is applied to each of the points.

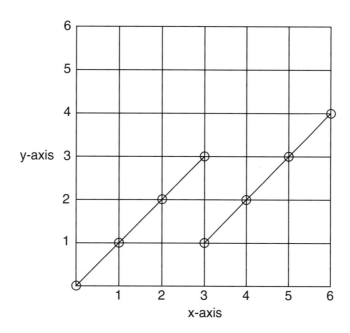

The point set {(0,0), (1,1), (2,2), (3,3)} is translated into the set {(3,1), (4,2), (5,3), (6,4)} by adding 3 to each x-value ($\Delta x = 3$) and 1 to each y-value ($\Delta y = 1$).

Step 1: Implement the `isTranslation` operation and add it to the file *ptlist.cpp*. A prototype for this operation is included in the declaration of the PointList class in the file *ptlist.h*.

Step 2: Add your implementation of the `isTranslation` operation to the file *ptlist.cpp*.

Step 3: Activate the 'T' (test translation) and '*' (insert into translation test list) commands in the test program *test2.cpp* by removing the comment delimiter (and the character '2') from the lines that begin with "//2".

Step 4: Complete the following test plan by adding test cases that check whether your implementation of the `isTranslation` operator correctly determines whether one PointList represents a translation of the other.

Step 5: Execute your test plan. If you discover mistakes in your implementation of the `isTranslation` operation, correct them and execute your test plan again.

Test Plan for the `isTranslation` Operation

PointList 1	PointList 2	$(\Delta x, \Delta y)$	Expected Result	Checked
(0,0) (1,1) (2,2)	(1,0) (2,1) (3,2)	(1,0)	True	

Laboratory 2: In-lab Exercise 3

Name _____   Date _____

Section _____

Inserting points at the beginning of a point list is a little bit trickier—and more time consuming—than adding them at the end.

```
void insertAtBeginning ( Point newPoint )
```

Requirements:
List is not full.

Results:
Inserts newPoint at the beginning of a list. If the list is empty, then inserts newPoint as the first (and only) point in the list. In either case, moves the cursor to newPoint.

Step 1: Implement this operation and add it to the file *ptlist.cpp*. A prototype for this operation is included in the declaration of the PointList class in the file *ptlist.h*.

Step 2: Activate the '#' (insert at beginning) command in the test program *test2.cpp* by removing the comment delimiter (and the character '3') from the lines beginning with "//3".

Step 3: Complete the following test plan by adding test cases that check whether your implementation of the insertAtBeginning operation correctly inserts points into an empty list.

Step 4: Execute your test plan. If you discover mistakes in your implementation of the insertAtBeginning operation, correct them and execute your test plan again.

Test Plan for the insertAtBeginning Operation

Test Case	Commands	Expected Result	Checked
Insert a series of points at the beginning of the list	# 1 2 # 3 4 # 5 6 # 7 8	(7,8) (5,6) (3,4) (1,2)	

Note: The point marked by the cursor is shown in **bold**.

Laboratory 2: Postlab Exercise 1

Name _____ Date _____

Section _____

Part A

Does hard-coding the maximum size of the point array `points` in the *ptlist.h* file cause any problems? Explain why or why not.

Part B

If it does cause problems, what would you do to overcome the problems?

Laboratory 2: Postlab Exercise 2

Name _____   Date _____

Section _____

Part A

Would the Point List ADT be harder to interact with if there were no cursor?

Part B

If you had no cursor, what changes would need to be made to the class?

Array Implementation of the List ADT

In this laboratory you will:

- Implement the List ADT using an array representation of a list, including development of an iteration scheme that allows you to move through a list data item by data item

- Create a program that analyzes the genetic content of a DNA sequence

- Analyze the efficiency of your array implementation of the List ADT

Overview

The list is one of the most frequently used data structures. Although all programs share the same definition of list—a sequence of homogeneous data items—the type of data item stored in lists varies from program to program. Some use lists of integers, others use lists of characters, floating-point numbers, points, and so forth. You normally have to decide on the data item type when you implement the ADT. If you need a different data item type, there are several possibilities.

1. You could edit the class code (the declaration file, *classname.h*, and the definition file, *classname.cpp*—in this case of the List ADT, *listarr.h* and *listarr.cpp*) and replace every reference to the old data type by the new data type. This is a lot of work, tedious, and error-prone.
2. A simpler solution is to use a made up data type name throughout the class, such as `DataType`, and then use the C++ `typedef` statement at the beginning of the class declaration file to specify what `DataType` really is. To specify that the list data items should be characters, you would type

    ```
    typedef char DataType;
    ```

    This approach does work, and changing the data item type is much easier than the first solution. We will be using this approach for the List ADT and the Ordered List ADT.

    This approach does, however, have drawbacks. A major problem with this method is that a given program can have `DataType` set to only one particular type. For instance, you cannot have both a list of characters and a list of integers; `DataType` must be either `char` or `int`. You could make separate copies of the List ADT and define `DataType` differently in each copy. Because you cannot have multiple classes in a program with the same name, you would also need to change every occurrence of the class name `List` to something like `CharList` or `IntList`. This works, but it gets messy and the whole process must be repeated every time you need a list with a new data item data type.
3. Fortunately, C++ has a third solution, **templates**, which we will explain in the Stack ADT in Laboratory 5. When using templates, you do not need to create a different list implementation for each type of list data item. Instead, you create a list implementation in terms of list data items of some **generic** type rather like solution 2 above. We will use the arbitrary string "DT" for the data type. This requires just one copy of the class code. You can then ask the compiler to make any number of lists in which the data items are an arbitrary data type by adding a simple piece of information when you declare a list in your code.

    ```
    List<int> samples;    // Create a list of integers
    List<char> line;      // Then create a list of characters
    ```

    We will return to templates in the Stack ADT.

If an ADT is to be useful, its operations must be both expressive and intuitive. The following List ADT provides operations that allow you to insert data items in a list, remove data items from a list, check the state of a list (is it empty, or is it full?), and iterate through the data items in a list. Iteration is done using a **cursor** that you move through the list much as you move the cursor in a text editor or word processor. In the following example, the List ADT's gotoBeginning operation is used to move the cursor to the beginning of the list. The cursor is then moved through the list data item by data item by repeated applications of the gotoNext operation. Note that the data item marked by the cursor is shown in bold.

After gotoBeginning: **a**   b   c   d

After gotoNext: a   **b**   c   d

After gotoNext: a   b   **c**   d

After gotoNext: a   b   c   **d**

List ADT

Data Items

The data items in a list are of generic type DataType.

Structure

The data items form a linear structure in which list data items follow one after the other, from the beginning of the list to its end. The ordering of the data items is determined by when and where each data item is inserted into the list and is *not* a function of the data contained in the list data items. At any point in time, one data item in any nonempty list is marked using the list's cursor. You travel through the list using operations that change the position of the cursor.

Operations

```
List ( int maxNumber = defMaxListSize ) throw ( bad_alloc )
```

Requirements:
None

Results:
Constructor. Creates an empty list. Allocates enough memory for a list containing maxNumber data items.

```
~List ()
```

Requirements:
None

Results:
Destructor. Deallocates (frees) the memory used to store a list.

```
void insert ( const DataType &newDataItem ) throw ( logic_error )
```

Requirements:
List is not full.

Results:
Inserts `newDataItem` into a list. If the list is not empty, then inserts `newDataItem` after the cursor. Otherwise, inserts `newDataItem` as the first (and only) data item in the list. In either case, moves the cursor to `newDataItem`.

```
void remove () throw ( logic_error )
```

Requirements:
List is not empty.

Results:
Removes the data item marked by the cursor from a list. If the resulting list is not empty, the cursor should now be marking the data item that followed the deleted data

item. If the deleted data item was at the end of the list, then moves the cursor to the data item at the beginning of the list.

```
void replace ( const DataType &newDataItem ) throw ( logic_error )
```

Requirements:
List is not empty.

Results:
Replaces the data item marked by the cursor with `newDataItem`. The cursor remains at `newDataItem`.

```
void clear ()
```

Requirements:
None

Results:
Removes all the data items in a list.

```
bool isEmpty () const
```

Requirements:
None

Results:
Returns `true` if a list is empty. Otherwise, returns `false`.

```
bool isFull () const
```

Requirements:
None

Results:
Returns `true` if a list is full. Otherwise, returns `false`.

```
void gotoBeginning () throw ( logic_error )
```

Requirements:
List is not empty.

Results:
If a list is not empty, then moves the cursor to the data item at the beginning of the list.

```
void gotoEnd () throw ( logic_error )
```

Requirements:
List is not empty.

Results:
If a list is not empty, then moves the cursor to the data item at the end of the list.

```
bool gotoNext () throw ( logic_error )
```

Requirements:
List is not empty.

Results:
If the cursor is not at the end of a list, then moves the cursor to the next data item in the list and returns `true`. Otherwise, returns `false`.

```
bool gotoPrior () ( logic_error )
```

Requirements:
List is not empty.

Results:
If the cursor is not at the beginning of a list, then moves the cursor to the preceding data item in the list and returns `true`. Otherwise, returns `false`.

```
DataType getCursor () const throw ( logic_error )
```

Requirements:
List is not empty.

Results:
Returns a copy of the data item marked by the cursor.

```
void showStructure () const
```

Requirements:
None

Results:
Outputs the data items in a list. If the list is empty, outputs "Empty list". Note that this operation is intended for testing/debugging purposes only. It only supports list data items that are one of C++'s predefined data types (`int`, `char`, and so forth).

Laboratory 3: Cover Sheet

Name _____ Date _____

Section _____

Place a check mark in the *Assigned* column next to the exercises your instructor has assigned to you. Attach this cover sheet to the front of the packet of materials you submit following the laboratory.

Activities	Assigned: Check or list exercise numbers	Completed
Prelab Exercise		
Bridge Exercise		
In-lab Exercise 1		
In-lab Exercise 2		
In-lab Exercise 3		
Postlab Exercise 1		
Postlab Exercise 2		
Total		

Laboratory 3: Prelab Exercise

Name _____   Date _____

Section _____

You can implement a list in many ways. Given that all the data items in a list are of the same type, and that the list structure is linear, an array seems a natural choice. You could declare the size of the array at **compile-time** (as you did with the logbook array in Laboratory 1), but your List ADT will be more flexible if you specify the size of the array at **run-time** and **dynamically allocate** the memory required to store it.

Memory allocation for the array is done by the **constructor**. The constructor is invoked whenever a list declaration is encountered during the execution of a program. Once called, the constructor allocates an array using C++'s `new` operator. The constructor outlined below, for example, allocates an array of `maxNumber` data items and assigns the address of the array to the pointer `dataItems`, where `dataItems` is of type `DataType*`.

```
List:: List ( int maxNumber )
{
    . . .
    dataItems = new DataType[maxNumber];
}
```

Whenever you allocate memory, you must ensure that it is deallocated when it is no longer needed. The **destructor** is used to deallocate the memory storing the array. This function is invoked whenever a list is destroyed—that is, if the function containing the corresponding list declaration terminates or if the list is explicitly destroyed by the programmer. The fact that the call to the destructor is made automatically eliminates the possibility of you forgetting to deallocate the list. The destructor outlined below frees the memory used by the array that you allocated above.

```
List:: ~List ()
{
    delete [] dataItems;
}
```

Another significant implementation issue is what to do when a logbook function such as `insert()` or `remove()` is called with parameters or preconditions that do not meet the stated requirements. Using the `remove()` function as an example, it is a logic error to request removal of an item from an empty list. Although there are many possible ways of dealing with this situation, the standard C++ method for dealing with bad parameters and other difficult—or impossible—situations is to `throw` an **exception**. Throwing an exception causes the currently active function to stop execution and return to the calling function. Unless that function or one of its callers takes special steps to handle the exception, the program will be halted. By using the C++ try and catch instructions, callers can decide what to do when an exception is thrown. The `try` instruction is used when trying something that might cause an exception. The `catch` instruction is used to specify what to do if an exception did occur inside the preceding try code block. Common catch responses to an exception include one or more of the following: 1) print out a helpful explanation of what went wrong, 2) try to work around the problem, and 3) halt the program. The empty list problem in the `remove()` function example can be dealt with by using the following code snippet at the beginning of the function to enforce the "List is not empty" requirement.

```
if ( size == 0 )
        throw logic_error("Remove: list is empty");
```

The C++ exception handling mechanism is quite complicated. For the purposes of this book, you will almost always be throwing a `logic_error` exception or one of just a few other exception types. We have written a longer discussion of exceptions and program validation techniques in Appendix 1. Please read it before completing Laboratory 3.

Also, note that for the purpose of demonstrating the usefulness of exceptions, we have included catch statements in the *test3.cpp* program to handle any exceptions that are thrown. This is the only test program that uses them heavily because they tend to clutter the code and make it less readable. We decided not to sacrifice the readability of the rest of our small test programs by adding complete error-handling capabilities. However, these capabilities are mandatory in large complex programs.

Step 1: Implement the operations in the List ADT using an array to store the list data items. Lists change in size; therefore, you need to store the maximum number of data items the list can hold (`maxSize`) and the actual number of data items in the list (`size`), along with the list data items themselves (`dataItems`). You also need to keep track of the array index (`cursor`). Base your implementation on the following declarations from the file *listarr.h*. An implementation of the showStructure operation is given in the file *show3.cpp*.

```
const int defMaxListSize = 10;    // Default maximum list size

typedef char DataType;

class List
{
  public:

    // Constructor
    List ( int maxNumber = defMaxListSize ) throw ( bad_alloc );

    // Destructor
    ~List ();

    // List manipulation operations
    void insert ( const DataType &newDataItem )    // Insert after cursor
        throw ( logic_error );
    void remove () throw ( logic_error );          // Remove data item
    void replace ( const DataType &newDataItem )   // Replace data item
        throw ( logic_error );
    void clear ();                                 // Clear list

    // List status operations
    bool isEmpty () const;                         // List is empty
    bool isFull () const;                          // List is full

    // List iteration operations
    void gotoBeginning () throw ( logic_error );   // Go to beginning
    void gotoEnd () throw ( logic_error );         // Go to end
```

```
bool gotoNext () throw ( logic_error );      // Go to next data item
bool gotoPrior () throw ( logic_error );     // Go to prior data item
DataType getCursor () const throw ( logic_error ); // Return data item

// Output the list structure – used in testing/debugging
void showStructure () const;

private:

// Data members
int maxSize,
    size,              // Actual number of data item in the list
    cursor;            // Cursor array index
DataType *dataItems;   // Array containing the list data item
};
```

Step 2: Save your implementation of the List ADT in the file *listarr.cpp*. Be sure to document your code.

The code in the file *listarr.cpp* provides a template (or framework) for a set of implementations of the List ADT. The type of the list data items is deliberately left unspecified in this framework and is only made specific where the data type is declared in the class declaration in *listarr.h*.

The following program uses the array implementation of the operations in the List ADT to read in a list of integer samples and compute their sum.

```
// For this example, set DataType to "int" in listarr.h.

#include <iostream>
#include "listarr.h"   // Include the class declaration file

using namespace std;

void main ()
{
    List samples(100);      // Set of samples
    int newSample,          // Input sample
        total = 0;          // Sum of the input samples

    // Read in a set of samples from the keyboard.

    cout << "Enter list of samples (end with eof) : ";
    while ( cin >> newSample )
        samples.insert(newSample);

    // Sum the samples and output the result.

    if ( !samples.isEmpty() )               // Verify that list has data
    {
        samples.gotoBeginning();            // Go to beginning of list
        do
            total += samples.getCursor();   // Add element to running sum
        while ( samples.gotoNext() );       // Go to next element (if any)
    }

    cout << "Sum is " << total << endl;
}
```

Laboratory 3: Bridge Exercise

Name _____ Date _____

Section _____

Check with your instructor whether you are to complete this exercise prior to your lab period or during lab.

The test programs that you used in Laboratory 1 consisted of a series of tests that were hard-coded into the programs. Adding a new test case to this style of test program requires changing the test program itself. In this and subsequent laboratories, you use a more flexible kind of test program to evaluate your ADT implementations, one in which you specify a test case using commands, rather than code. These interactive, command-driven test programs allow you to check a new test case by simply entering a series of keyboard commands and observing the results.

The test program in the file *test3.cpp*, for instance, supports the following commands.

Command	Action
+x	Insert data item x after the cursor.
-	Remove the data item marked by the cursor.
=x	Replace the data item marked by the cursor with data item x.
@	Display the data item marked by the cursor.
N	Go to the next data item.
P	Go to the prior data item.
<	Go to the beginning of the list.
>	Go to the end of the list.
E	Report whether the list is empty.
F	Report whether the list is full.
C	Clear the list.
Q	Quit the test program.

Suppose you wish to confirm that your array implementation of the List ADT successfully inserts a data item into a list that has been emptied by a series of calls to the remove operation. You can test this case by entering the following sequence of keyboard commands.

Command	+a	+b	-	-	+c	Q
Action	Insert a	Insert b	Remove	Remove	Insert c	Quit

It is easy to see how this interactive test program allows you to rapidly examine a variety of test cases. This speed comes with a price, however. You must be careful not to violate the preconditions required by the operations that you are testing. For instance, the commands

Command	+a	+b	-	-	-
Action	Insert a	Insert b	Remove	Remove	Error (exception)

cause the test program to fail during the last call to the remove operation. The source of the failure does not lie in the implementation of the List ADT, nor is the test program flawed. The failure occurs because this sequence of operations creates a state that violates the preconditions of the remove operation (the list must *not* be empty when the remove operation is invoked). The speed with which you can create and evaluate test cases using an interactive, command-driven test program makes it very easy to produce this kind of error. It is very tempting to just sit down and start entering commands. A much better strategy, however, is to create a test plan, listing the test cases you wish to check and then to write out command sequences that generate these test cases. Of course, you should also deliberately violate function requirements in order to test your exception handling.

Step 1: Compile and link the test program in the file *test3.cpp*. Note that when compiling this program you need to ensure that `DataType` is defined as `char` and that you also compile and link in your array implementation of the List ADT (in the file *listarr.cpp*) to produce the correct executable for a list of characters.

Step 2: Complete the following test plan by adding test cases that check whether your implementation of the List ADT correctly handles the following tasks:

- Insertions into a newly emptied list
- Insertions that fill a list to its maximum size
- Deletions from a full list
- Determining whether a list is empty
- Determining whether a list is full

Assume that the output of one test case is used as the input to the following test case, and note that although expected results are listed for the final command in each command sequence, you should confirm that *each* command produces a correct result.

Step 3: Execute your test plan. If you discover mistakes in your implementation of the List ADT, correct them and execute your test plan again.

Test Plan for the Operations in the List ADT

Test Case	Commands	Expected Result	Checked
Insert at end	+a +b +c +d	a b c **d**	
Travel from beginning	< N N	a b **c** d	
Travel from end	> P P	a **b** c d	
Delete middle data item	-	a **c** d	
Insert in middle	+e +f +f	a c e f **f** d	
Remove last data item	> -	a c e f **f**	
Remove first data item	< -	**c** e f f	
Display data item	@	Returns c	
Replace data item	=g	**g** e f f	
Clear the list	C	Empty list	

Note: The data item marked by the cursor is shown in **bold**.

Step 4: Change the list in the test program from a list of characters to a list of integers by replacing the declaration for `DataType` in *listarr.h* and `testDataItem` in *test3.cpp* with

```
typedef int DataType;
int testDataItem;    // List data item
```

Step 5: Recompile and relink the test program. Note that recompiling the program will compile your implementation of the List ADT (in the file *listarr.cpp*) to produce an implementation for a list of integers.

Step 6: Replace the character data in your test plan ('a' to 'g') with integer values.

Step 7: Execute your revised test plan using the revised test program. If you discover mistakes in your implementation of the List ADT, correct them and execute your revised test plan again.

Laboratory 3: In-lab Exercise 1

Name _____   Date _____

Section _____

The genetic information encoded in a strand of deoxyribonucleic acid (DNA) is stored in the purine and pyrimidine bases (adenine, guanine, cytosine, and thymine) that form the strand. Biologists are keenly interested in the bases in a DNA sequence because these bases determine what the sequence does.

By convention, DNA sequences are represented using lists containing the letters A, G, C, and T (for adenine, guanine, cytosine, and thymine, respectively). The following function computes one property of a DNA sequence—the number of times each base occurs in the sequence.

```
void countBases ( List &dnaSequence, int &aCount,
                  int &cCount, int &tCount, int &gCount )
```

Input Parameters:
dnaSequence: contains the bases in a DNA sequence encoded using the characters A, C, T, and G.

Output Parameters:
aCount, cCount, tCount, gCount: the number of times the corresponding base appears in the DNA sequence.

Step 1: Implement this function and add it to the program in the file *test3dna.cpp*. Your implementation should manipulate the DNA sequence using the operations in the List ADT. A prototype for this function is given in the file *test3dna.cpp*.

Step 2: The program in the file *test3dna.cpp* reads a DNA sequence from the keyboard, calls the countBases() function, and outputs the resulting base counts. Complete the following test plan by adding DNA sequences of different lengths and various combinations of bases.

Step 3: Execute your test plan. If you discover mistakes in your implementation of the countBases() function, correct them and execute your test plan again.

Test Plan for the countBases() Function

Test Case	DNA Sequence	Expected Result	Checked
Sequence with 10 bases	AGTACATGTA	aCount = 4 cCount = 1 tCount = 3 gCount = 2	

Laboratory 3: In-lab Exercise 2

Name _____   Date _____

Section _____

In many applications, the ordering of the data items in a list changes over time. Not only are new data items added and existing ones removed, but data items are repositioned within the list. The following List ADT operation moves a data item to a new position in a list.

```
void moveToNth ( int n ) throw ( logic_error )
```

Requirements:
List contains at least n+1 data items.

Results:
Removes the data item marked by the cursor from a list and reinserts it as the *n*th data item in the list, where the data items are numbered from beginning to end, starting with zero. Moves the cursor to the moved data item.

Step 1: Implement this operation and add it to the file *listarr.cpp*. A prototype for this operation is included in the declaration of the List class in the file *listarr.h*.

Step 2: Activate the 'M' (move) command in the test program *test3.cpp* by removing the comment delimiter (and the character 'M') from the lines that begin with "//M".

Step 3: Complete the following test plan by adding test cases that check whether your implementation of the moveToNth operation correctly processes moves within full and single data item lists.

Step 4: Execute your test plan. If you discover mistakes in your implementation of the moveToNth operation, correct them and execute your test plan again.

Test Plan for the moveToNth Operation

Test Case	Commands	Expected Result	Checked
Set up list	+a +b +c +d	a b c d	
Move first data item	< M2	b c **a** d	
Move data item back	M0	**a** b c d	
Move to end of list	M3	b c d **a**	
Move back one	M2	b c **a** d	
Move forward one	M3	b c d **a**	

Note: The data item marked by the cursor is shown in **bold**.

Laboratory 3: In-lab Exercise 3

Name _____   Date _____

Section _____

Finding a particular list data item is another very common task. The following operation searches a list for a specified data item. The fact that the search begins with the data item marked by the cursor—and not at the beginning of the list—means that this operation can be applied iteratively to locate all of the occurrences of a specified data item.

```
bool find ( const DataType &searchDataItem ) throw ( logic_error )
```

Requirements:
List is not empty.

Results:
Searches a list for `searchDataItem`. Begins the search with the data item marked by the cursor. Moves the cursor through the list until either `searchDataItem` is found (returns `true`) or the end of the list is reached without finding `searchDataItem` (returns `false`). Leaves the cursor at the last data item visited during the search.

Step 1: Implement this operation and add it to the file *listarr.cpp*. A prototype for this operation is included in the declaration of the List class in the file *listarr.h*.

Step 2: Activate the '?' (find) command in the test program *test4.cpp* by removing the comment delimiter (and the character '?') from the lines that begin with "//?".

Step 3: Complete the following test plan by adding test cases that check whether your implementation of the `find` operation correctly conducts searches in full lists, as well as searches that begin with the last data item in a list.

Step 4: Execute your test plan. If you discover mistakes in your implementation of the `find` operation, correct them and execute your test plan again.

Test Plan for the `find` Operation

Test Case	Commands	Expected Result	Checked
Set up list	+a +b +c +a	a b c **a**	
Successful search	< ?a	Search succeeds	
		a b c a	
Search for duplicate	N ?a	Search succeeds	
		a b c **a**	
Successful search	< ?b	Search succeeds	
		a **b** c a	
Search for duplicate	N ?b	Search fails	
		a b c a	

Note: The data item marked by the cursor is shown in **bold**.

Laboratory 3: Postlab Exercise 1

Name _____   Date _____

Section _____

Given a list containing N data items, develop worst-case, order-of-magnitude estimates of the execution time of the following List ADT operations, assuming they are implemented using an array. Briefly explain your reasoning behind each estimate.

insert   O(   )
Explanation:

remove   O(   )
Explanation:

gotoNext   O(   )

Explanation:

gotoPrior   O(   )

Explanation:

Laboratory 3: Postlab Exercise 2

Name _____ Date _____

Section _____

Part A

Give a declaration—including `typedef`—for a list of floating-point numbers called `echoReadings`. Assume that the list can contain no more than fifty floating-point numbers.

Part B

Give the declarations—including `typedef`—required for a list of (*x*,*y*,*z*)-coordinates called `coords`. Assume that *x*, *y*, and *z* are floating-point numbers and that there will be no more than twenty coordinates in the list.

Part C

Are the declarations you created in Parts A and B compatible with the operations in your implementation of the List ADT? Briefly explain why or why not.

Ordered List ADT

In this laboratory you will:

- Implement the Ordered List ADT using an array to store the list data items and a binary search to locate data items

- Use inheritance to derive a new class from an existing one

- Create a program that reassembles a message that has been divided into packets

- Use ordered lists to create efficient merge and subset operations

- Analyze the efficiency of your implementation of the Ordered List ADT

Overview

In an **ordered list** the data items are maintained in ascending (or descending) order based on the data contained in the list data items. Typically, the contents of one field are used to determine the ordering. This field is referred to as the **key field**, or the **key**. In this laboratory, we assume that each data item in an ordered list has a key that uniquely identifies the data item—that is, no two data items in any ordered list have the same key. As a result, you can use a data item's key to efficiently retrieve the data item from a list.

Ordered List ADT

Data Items

The data items in an ordered list are of generic type DataType. Each data item has a key (of type `char`) that uniquely identifies the data item. Data items usually include additional data. Type DataType must provide a function called `getKey()` that returns a data item's key.

Structure

The list data items are stored in ascending order based on their keys. For each list data item *E,* the data item that precedes *E* has a key that is less than *E*'s key, and the data item that follows *E* has a key that is greater than *E*'s key. At any point in time, one data item in any nonempty list is marked using the list's cursor. You travel through the list using operations that change the position of the cursor.

Operations

```
List ( int maxNumber = defMaxListSize ) throw ( bad_alloc )
```

Requirements:
None

Results:
Constructor. Creates an empty list. Allocates enough memory for a list containing maxNumber data items.

```
~List ()
```

Requirements:
None

Results:
Destructor. Deallocates (frees) the memory used to store a list.

```
void insert ( const DataType &newDataItem ) throw ( logic_error )
```

Requirements:
List is not full.

Results:
Inserts newDataItem in its appropriate position within a list. If a data item with the same key as newDataItem already exists in the list, then updates that data item's nonkey fields with newDataItem's nonkey fields. Moves the cursor to mark newDataItem.

```
bool retrieve ( char searchKey, DataType &searchDataItem ) const
```

Requirements:
None

Results:
Searches a list for the data item with key searchKey. If the data item is found, then moves the cursor to the data item, copies it to searchDataItem, and returns true. Otherwise, returns false without moving the cursor and with searchDataItem undefined.

```
void remove () throw ( logic_error )
```

Requirements:
List is not empty.

Results:
Removes the data item marked by the cursor from a list. If the resulting list is not empty, then moves the cursor to the data item that followed the deleted data item. If the deleted data item was at the end of the list, then moves the cursor to the beginning of the list.

```
void replace ( const DataType &newDataItem ) throw ( logic_error )
```

Requirements:
List is not empty.

Results:
Replaces the data item marked by the cursor with newDataItem. Note that this entails removing the data item and inserting newDataItem. Moves the cursor to newDataItem.

```
void clear ()
```

Requirements:
None

Results:
Removes all the data items in a list.

```
bool isEmpty () const
```

Requirements:
None

Results:
Returns true if a list is empty. Otherwise, returns false.

```
bool isFull () const
```

Requirements:
None

Results:
Returns `true` if a list is full. Otherwise, returns `false`.

```
void gotoBeginning () throw ( logic_error )
```

Requirements:
List is not empty.

Results:
Moves the cursor to the data item at the beginning of the list.

```
void gotoEnd () throw ( logic_error )
```

Requirements:
List is not empty.

Results:
Moves the cursor to the data item at the end of the list.

```
bool gotoNext () throw ( logic_error )
```

Requirements:
List is not empty.

Results:
If the cursor is not at the end of a list, then moves the cursor to the next data item in the list and returns `true`. Otherwise, returns `false`.

```
bool gotoPrior () throw ( logic_error )
```

Requirements:
List is not empty.

Results:
If the cursor is not at the beginning of a list, then moves the cursor to the preceding data item in the list and returns `true`. Otherwise, returns `false`.

```
DataType getCursor () const throw ( logic_error )
```

Requirements:
List is not empty.

Results:
Returns a copy of the data item marked by the cursor.

```
void showStructure () const
```

Requirements:
None.

Results:
Outputs the keys of the data items in a list. If the list is empty, outputs "Empty list".
Note that this operation is intended for testing/debugging purposes only. It only
supports keys that are one of C++'s predefined data types (`int`, `char`, and so forth).

Laboratory 4: Cover Sheet

Name _____ Date _____

Section _____

Place a check mark in the *Assigned* column next to the exercises your instructor has assigned to you. Attach this cover sheet to the front of the packet of materials you submit following the laboratory.

Activities	Assigned: Check or list exercise numbers	Completed
Prelab Exercise		
Bridge Exercise		
In-lab Exercise 1		
In-lab Exercise 2		
In-lab Exercise 3		
Postlab Exercise 1		
Postlab Exercise 2		
Total		

Laboratory 4: Prelab Exercise

Name _____ Date _____

Section _____

There is a great deal of similarity between the Ordered List ADT and the List ADT. In fact, with the exception of the insert, retrieve, and replace operations, these ADTs are identical. Rather than implementing the Ordered List ADT from the ground up, you can take advantage of these similarities by using your array implementation of the List ADT from Laboratory 3 as a foundation for an array implementation of the Ordered List ADT.

A key feature of C++ is the ability to derive a new class from an existing one through **inheritance**. The **derived class** inherits the member functions and data members of the existing **base class** and can have its own member functions and data members as well. The following declaration from the file *ordlist.h* derives a class called OrdList from the List class.

```
class OrdList : public List
{
  public:

    // Constructor
    OrdList ( int maxNumber = defMaxListSize );

    // Modified (or new) list manipulation operations
    virtual void insert ( const DataType &newDataItem )
        throw ( logic_error );
    virtual void replace ( const DataType &newDataItem )
        throw ( logic_error );
    bool retrieve ( char searchKey, DataType &searchDataItem );

    // Output the list structure — used in testing/debugging
    void showStructure () const;

  private:

    // Locates a data item (or where it should be) based on its key
    bool binarySearch ( char searchKey, int &index );
};
```

The declaration

```
class OrdList : public List
```

indicates that OrdList is derived from List. The keyword "public" specifies that this is a **public inheritance**—that is, OrdList inherits access to List's public member functions, but not to its private data members (or private member functions).

You want the member functions in OrdList to be able to refer to List's private data members, so you must change the data members in the List class declaration from private to protected, as follows.

```
class List
{
   ...

  protected:

    // Data members
    int maxSize,           // Maximum number of data items in the list
        size,              // Actual number of data items in the list
        cursor;            // Cursor array index
    DataType *dataItems;   // Array containing the list data items
};
```

In a public inheritance, private List data members can only be accessed by List member functions. Protected List data members, on the other hand, can be accessed by the member functions in any class that is derived from List: OrdList, in this case.

The OrdList class supplies its own constructor, as well as a pair of new member functions: a public member function retrieve() that retrieves a data item based on its key, and a private member facilitator function binarySearch() that locates a data item in the array using a binary search. The OrdList class also includes its own versions of the insert() and replace() public member functions. The redefinition of these functions is indicated by the use of the keyword virtual in their function prototypes. Note that you must change this pair of functions to virtual in the List class declaration as well.

```
class List
{
  public:

    ...
    // List manipulation operations
    virtual void insert ( const DataType &newDataItem )   // Insert
        throw ( logic_error );
    virtual void replace ( const DataType &newDataItem ) // Replace
        throw ( logic_error );
    ...

  protected:

    // Data members
    int maxSize,           // Maximum number of data items in the list
        size,              // Actual number of data items in the list
        cursor;            // Cursor array index
    DataType *dataItems;   // Array containing the list data items
};
```

A class declaration for the List class containing the changes specified above is given in the file *listarr2.h*.

An OrdList object can call any of the List public member functions, as well as any of its own member functions. The following program reads in the account number and balance for a set of accounts and outputs the accounts in ascending order based on their account numbers.

```cpp
#include <iostream>

struct DataType
{
    int acctNum;            // (Key) Account number
    float balance;          // Account balance

    int getKey () const
        { return acctNum; }    // Returns the key
};

#include "ordlist.cpp"

const int maxNameLength = 15;

void main()
{
    OrdList accounts;        // List of accounts
    DataType acct;           // A single account

    // Read in information on a set of accounts.

    cout << endl << "Enter account information (EOF to end) : "
        << endl;
    while ( cin >> acct.acctNum >> acct.balance )
        accounts.insert(acct);

    // Output the accounts in ascending order based on their account
    // numbers.

    cout << endl;
    if ( !accounts.isEmpty() )
    {
        accounts.gotoBeginning();
        do
        {
            acct = accounts.getCursor();
            cout << acct.acctNum << " " << acct.balance << endl;
        }
        while ( accounts.gotoNext() );
    }
};
```

The Account structure includes a getKey() function that returns an account's key field—its account number. This function is used by the OrdList class to order the accounts as they are inserted. Insertion is done using the OrdList class insert() function, but list traversal is done using the inherited List class gotoBeginning() and gotoNext() functions.

Another change from the Laboratory 3 List class implementation is that we will not use typedef any more. We just declare a struct or class in the application program (see preceding example) and name it DataType. To ensure that the code in the OrdList class and in the List class have access to the type information, we include the file *ordlist.cpp*—instead of *ordlist.h*—near the start of the application program on a line below where `DataType` is declared. This goes against the principles of modular coding, but it simplifies the implementation. Furthermore, we will need to use this approach when we implement the next laboratory, the Stack ADT, using C++ templates.

We are introducing one more C++ programming technique that helps avoid the accidental—and sometimes unavoidable—multiple inclusion of class implementation files. For instance, assume that an application program needs ordered lists. It includes the OrdList class, which in turn includes the List class. The programmer might now include another class derived from the List class. The result is that the compiler encounters the List class implementation twice and signals an error. The solution is to use the C++ preprocessor to enable **conditional compilation**. Conditional compilation allows the programmer to control what parts of a file the compiler will try to compile. In this case, we ensure that the compiler only tries to compile the contents of each file once, regardless of how many times the file has been included.

We protect *ordlist.h* by inserting three lines around the entire code contents of the file as follows:

```
#ifndef ORDLIST_H
#define ORDLIST_H

...        // The previous contents of the file

#endif
```

The line "`#ifndef ORDLIST_H`" means that if the string "`ORDLIST_H`" has not yet been defined, then compile all the code up to the matching "`#endif`" line. The first thing that happens within that block is that the identifier `ORDLIST_H` is defined. If the compiler encounters the file again during that compilation, `ORDLIST_H` will be already defined and all code up through the `#endif` will be ignored. The tradition for identifier names is that they should match the file name. The period character ('.') is not valid for identifiers, so it is replaced by the underscore ('_') character. Conditional compilation by means of C++ preprocessor definitions becomes progressively more useful as programs become larger and more complex.

Step 1: The `showStructure()` and `find()` functions from your array implementation of the List ADT are designed for use with lists that are composed of one of C++'s built-in types. Comment out these functions and save the resulting implementation of the List ADT in the file *listarr2.cpp*.

Step 2: Implement the operations in the Ordered List ADT using the array representation of a list. Base your implementation on the following declaration from the file *ordlist.h*.

```
#include "listarr2.cpp"

class OrdList : public List
{
  public:

    // Constructor
    OrdList ( int maxNumber = defMaxListSize );
```

```
    // Modified (or new) list manipulation operations
    virtual void insert ( const DataType &newDataItem )
        throw ( logic_error );
    virtual void replace ( const DataType &newDataItem )
        throw ( logic_error );
    bool retrieve ( char searchKey, DataType &searchDataItem );

    // Output the list structure -- used in testing/debugging
    void showStructure () const;

  private:

    // Locates a data item (or where it should be) based on its key
    bool binarySearch ( char searchKey, int &index );
};
```

Note that you only need to create implementations of the constructor, insert, replace, and retrieve operations for the Ordered List ADT–the remainder of the operations are inherited from your array implementation of the List ADT. Your implementations of the insert and retrieve operations should use the `binarySearch()` function to locate a data item. An implementation of the binary search algorithm is given in the file *search.cpp*. An implementation of the `showStructure` operation is given in the file *show4.cpp*.

Step 3: Save your implementation of the Ordered List ADT in the file *ordlist.cpp*. Be sure to document your code.

Laboratory 4: Bridge Exercise

Name _____   Date _____

Section _____

Check with your instructor whether you are to complete this exercise prior to your lab period or during lab.

The test program in the file *test4.cpp* allows you to interactively test your implementation of the Ordered List ADT using the following commands.

Command	Action
+key	Insert (or update) the data item with the specified key.
?key	Retrieve the data item with the specified key and output it.
-	Remove the data item marked by the cursor.
@	Display the data item marked by the cursor.
=key	Replace the data item marked by the cursor.
N	Go to the next data item.
P	Go to the prior data item.
<	Go to the beginning of the list.
>	Go to the end of the list.
E	Report whether the list is empty.
F	Report whether the list is full.
C	Clear the list.
Q	Quit the test program.

Step 1: Prepare a test plan for your implementation of the Ordered List ADT. Your test plan should cover the application of each operation to data items at the beginning, middle, and end of lists (where appropriate). A test plan form follows.

Step 2: Execute your test plan. If you discover mistakes in your implementation, correct them and execute your test plan again.

Test Plan for the Operations in the Ordered List ADT

Test Case	Commands	Expected Result	Checked

Laboratory 4: In-lab Exercise 1

When a communications site transmits a message through a packet-switching network, it does not send the message as a continuous stream of data. Instead, it divides the message into pieces called **packets**. These packets are sent through the network to a receiving site, which reassembles the message. Packets may be transmitted to the receiving site along different paths. As a result, they are likely to arrive out of sequence. In order for the receiving site to reassemble the message correctly, each packet must include the relative position of the packet within the message.

For example, if we break the message "A SHORT MESSAGE" into packets five characters long and preface each packet with a number denoting the packet's position in the message, the result is the following set of packets.

```
1 A SHO
2 RT ME
3 SSAGE
```

No matter in what order these packets arrive, a receiving site can correctly reassemble the message by placing the packets in ascending order based on their position numbers.

Step 1: Create a program that reassembles the packets contained in a text file and outputs the corresponding message. Your program should use the Ordered List ADT to assist in reassembling the packets in a message. Assume that each packet in the message file contains a position number and five characters from the message (the packet format shown in the preceding paragraph). Base your program on the following declarations.

```cpp
const int packetSize = 6;   // Number of characters in a packet
                            // including null ('\0') terminator

struct DataType
{
    int position;            // Packet's position w/in the message
    char body[packetSize];   // Characters in the packet

    int key () const
        { return position; }   // Returns the key field
};
```

Store your program in the file *packet.cpp*.

Step 2: Test your program using the message in the text file *message.dat*.

Test Plan for the Message Processing Program

Test Case	Checked
Message in the file *message.dat*	

Laboratory 4: In-lab Exercise 2

Name _____ Date _____

Section _____

Suppose you wish to combine the data items in two ordered lists of similar size. You could use repeated calls to the insert operation to insert the data items from one list into the other. However, the resulting process would not be very efficient. A more effective approach is to use a specialized **merge** operation that takes advantage of the fact that the lists are ordered.

```
void merge ( const OrdList &fromL )
```

Requirements:
Lists have no keys in common.

Results:
Merges the data items in `fromL` into a list. Does not change `fromL`.

Even before you begin to merge the lists, you already know how much larger the list will become (remember, no key is in both lists). By traversing the lists in parallel, starting with their highest keys and working backward, you can perform the merge in a single pass. Given two ordered lists, alpha and beta, containing the keys

```
alpha : a d j t
beta  : b e w
```

the call

```
alpha.merge(beta);
```

produces the following results.

```
alpha : a b d e j t w
beta  : b e w
```

Step 1: Implement this operation and add it to the file *ordlist.cpp*. A prototype for this operation is included in the declaration of the Ordered List class in the file *ordlist.h*.

Step 2: Activate the 'M' (merge) command in the test program in the file *test4two.cpp* by removing the comment delimiter (and the character 'M') from the lines that begin with "//M".

Step 3: Prepare a test plan for the merge operation that covers lists of various lengths, including empty lists and lists that combine to produce a full list. A test plan form follows.

Step 4: Execute your test plan. If you discover mistakes in your implementation of the merge operation, correct them and execute your test plan again.

Test Plan for the Merge Operation

Test Case	Commands	Expected Result	Checked

Laboratory 4: In-lab Exercise 3

Name _____   Date _____

Section _____

A set of objects can be represented in many ways. If you use an unordered list to represent a set, then performing set operations such as intersection, union, difference, and subset requires up to $O(N^2)$ time. By using an ordered list to represent a set, however, you can reduce the execution time for these set operations to $O(N)$, a substantial improvement.

Consider the following subset operation. If the sets are stored as unordered lists, this operation requires that you traverse the list once for *each* data item in subL. But if the sets are stored as ordered lists, only a single traversal is required. The key is to move through the lists in parallel.

```
bool isSubset ( const OrdList &subL ) const
```

Requirements:
None

Results:
Returns `true` if every key in subL is also in a list. Otherwise, returns `false`.

Given three ordered lists, `alpha`, `beta`, and `gamma`, containing the keys

```
alpha : a b c d
beta  : a c x
gamma : a b
delta : <empty list>
```

the call `alpha.isSubset(beta)` yields the value `false` (beta is not a subset of `alpha`), the call `alpha.isSubset(gamma)` yields the value `true` (gamma is a subset of `alpha`), and the calls `alpha.isSubset(delta)` and `beta.isSubset(delta)` yield the value `true` (the empty set is a subset of every set).

Step 1: Implement this operation and add it to the file *ordlist.cpp*. A prototype for this operation is included in the declaration of the Ordered List class in the file *ordlist.h*.

Step 2: Activate the 'S' (subset) command in the test program in the file *test4two.cpp* by removing the comment delimiter (and the character 'S') from the lines that begin with "//S".

Step 3: Prepare a test plan for the subset operation that covers lists of various lengths, including empty lists. A test plan form follows.

Step 4: Execute your test plan. If you discover mistakes in your implementation of the subset operation, correct them and execute your test plan again.

Test Plan for the Subset Operation

Test Case	Commands	Expected Result	Checked

Laboratory 4: Postlab Exercise 1

Name _____   Date _____

Section _____

Part A

Given an ordered list containing N data items, develop worst-case, order-of-magnitude estimates of the execution time of the steps in the insert operation, assuming this operation is implemented using an array in conjunction with a binary search. Briefly explain your reasoning behind each estimate.

Array Implementation of the Insert Operation

Find the insertion point	O( )
Insert the data item	O( )
	_____
Entire operation	O( )

Explanation:

Part B

Suppose you had implemented the Ordered List ADT using a linear search rather than a binary search. Given an ordered list containing N data items, develop worst-case, order-of-magnitude estimates of the execution time of the steps in the insert operation. Briefly explain your reasoning behind each estimate.

Linked List Implementation of the Insert Operation

Find the insertion point   O(   )

     Insert the data item   O(   )

     Entire operation   O(   )

     Explanation:

Laboratory 4: Postlab Exercise 2

Name _____ Date _____

Section _____

In specifying the Ordered List ADT, we assumed that no two data items in an ordered list have the same key. What changes would you have to make to your implementation of the Ordered List ADT in order to support ordered lists in which multiple data items have the same key?

Stack ADT

Objectives

In this laboratory you will

■ Create two implementations of the Stack ADT—one based on an array representation of stack, the other based on a singly linked list representation

■ Use templates to produce a generic stack data structure

■ Create a program that evaluates arithmetic expressions in postfix form

■ Create a program that evaluates expressions for properly balanced pairs of parentheses and braces

■ Analyze the kinds of permutations you can produce using a stack

Overview

Many applications that use a linear data structure do not require the full range of operations supported by the List ADT. Although you can develop these applications using the List ADT, the resulting programs are likely to be somewhat cumbersome and inefficient. An alternative approach is to define new linear data structures that support more constrained sets of operations. By carefully defining these ADTs, you can produce ADTs that meet the needs of a diverse set of applications but yield data structures that are easier to apply–and are often more efficient–than the List ADT.

The **stack** is one example of a constrained linear data structure. In a stack, the data items are ordered from most recently added (the **top**) to least recently added (the **bottom**). All insertions and deletions are performed at the top of the stack. You use the **push** operation to insert a data item onto the stack and the **pop** operation to remove the topmost stack data item. A sequence of pushes and pops is shown below.

Push a	*Push* b	*Push* c	*Pop*	*Pop*
		c		
	b	b	b	
a	a	a	a	a
—	—	—	—	—

These constraints on insertion and deletion produce the "last in, first out" (LIFO) behavior that characterizes a stack. Although the stack data structure is narrowly defined, it is so extensively used by systems software that support for a primitive stack is one of the basic data items of most computer architectures.

The stack is one of the most frequently used data structures. Although all programs share the same definition of **stack**–a sequence of homogeneous data items with insertion and removal done at one end–the type of data items stored in stacks varies from program to program. Some use stacks of integers; others use stacks of characters, floating-point numbers, points, and so forth.

In Lab 3 you dealt with this problem by using the C++ `typedef` statement. That approach can be made to work, but it is laborious and error-prone. We mentioned that a better approach would be introduced here, in Lab 5.

That better approach is the C++ **template class.** A template is something that serves as a pattern. The pattern is not the final product, but is used to enable faster production of a final product. C++ template classes–of which the stack is an example– save you from needing to create a different stack implementation for each type of stack data item and from constantly playing with `typedef`. Instead, you create the stack implementation in terms of a **generic** data type. Every place in your code where you would normally have to specify the data type, you instead use an arbitrary string to represent any actual data type that you might later wish to use. We will use the arbitrary string "DT"–for *Data Type*–to represent the generic data type. Nowhere does either the class declaration (the *class.h* file) or the class definition (the *class.cpp* file) specify an actual C++ data type. You can defer specifying the actual data type until it is time to **instantiate** (create) an object of that class.

Following are a few simple rules for creating and using a template class.

- The string "`template < class DT >`" must go right before the class declaration and before every class member function. Remember, `DT` is our arbitrary identifier that will represent any data type in the template class. So the lines

```
class Stack
{
  public:
    . . .
```

are changed to

```
template < class DT >
class Stack
{
  public:
    . . .
```

The start of a function definition that used to be

```
Stack:: Stack ( int maxNumber ) throw ( bad_alloc )
```

now becomes

```
template < class DT >
Stack<DT>:: Stack ( int maxNumber ) throw ( bad_alloc )
```

Every use of the class name now must include the generic data type name enclosed in angle brackets. Every instance of the string "`Stack`" becomes "`Stack<DT>`". In the example constructor definition, the class resolution "`Stack::`" becomes "`Stack<DT>::`". Also note that the exception to the rule is that the constructor name is not modified—it remains just "`Stack`".

```
template < class DT >
Stack<DT>:: Stack ( int maxNumber ) throw ( bad_alloc )
```

- Every occurrence of the data type name inside the class declaration and definition files gets replaced by the string chosen to represent the generic data type. For instance, the line

```
int *dataItems;   // Array containing the stack data items
                  //  (integers)
```

becomes

```
DT *dataItems;    // Array containing the stack data items
                  //  (generic)
```

- When it is time to instantiate an object of that class, the real data type—inside angle brackets—is appended to the class name. So the lines

```
// A separate stack implementation just for integers
IntStack samples(10);

// Data type specified elsewhere by using typedef
Stack line(80);
```

now become

```
// We tell the compiler to make a copy of the generic stack just
// for integers and to make another just for characters.
Stack<int>  samples(10);
Stack<char> line(80);
```

- The code in the implementation file—the *classname.cpp* file—provides a template (or framework) for a set of implementations of the class ADT. The type of the data item is deliberately left unspecified in this framework and is not made specific until an object of the class is instantiated. As a result, the compiler must have access to the code in the .cpp file whenever it encounters a list declaration so that it can construct an implementation for the declared type of data item. Sophisticated program development environments provide a variety of mechanisms for ensuring access to this code. Unfortunately, these mechanisms are not yet standardized across systems. In this book you use a mechanism that is primitive but effective. You include the implementation file—*classname.cpp*—rather than the header file—*classname.h*—in any program that used this class. This approach violates the rule that you should never use a #include directive to include code. Most systems, however, provide no other means for using templated classes short of putting all the code for a program in one file (a much worse approach).

A partial template class declaration for the Stack ADT is shown below (the complete declaration is given in the Prelab Exercise).

```
template < class DT >
class Stack
{
  public:
    ...
    Stack ( int maxNumber = defMaxStackSize )      // Constructor
        throw ( bad_alloc );
    void push ( const DT &newDataItem )            // Push data item
        throw ( logic_error );
    DT pop ()                                      // Pop data item
        throw ( logic_error );
    ...
  private:
    ...
    DT *dataItems;  // Array containing the stack data items
};
```

Note the occurrences of the template parameter DT within the class declaration. This parameter is used to mark locations where explicit references are made to the stack data item type.

Stack ADT

Data items

The data items in a stack are of generic type DT.

Structure

The stack data items are linearly ordered from most recently added (the top) to least recently added (the bottom). Data items are inserted onto (pushed) and removed from (popped) the top of the stack.

Operations

```
Stack ( int maxNumber = defMaxStackSize ) throw ( bad_alloc )
```

Requirements:
None

Results:
Constructor. Creates an empty stack. Allocates enough memory for a stack containing maxNumber data items (if necessary).

```
~Stack ()
```

Requirements:
None

Results:
Destructor. Deallocates (frees) the memory used to store a stack.

```
void push ( const DT &newDataItem ) throw ( logic_error )
```

Requirements:
Stack is not full.

Results:
Inserts newDataItem onto the top of a stack.

```
DT pop () throw ( logic_error )
```

Requirements:
Stack is not empty.

Results:
Removes the most recently added (top) data item from a stack and returns it.

```
void clear ()
```

Requirements:
None

Results:
Removes all the data items in a stack.

```
bool isEmpty () const
```

Requirements:
None

Results:
Returns `true` if a stack is empty. Otherwise, returns `false`.

```
bool isFull () const
```

Requirements:
None

Results:
Returns `true` if a stack is full. Otherwise, returns `false`.

```
void showStructure () const
```

Requirements:
None

Results:
Outputs the data items in a stack. If the stack is empty, outputs "Empty stack". Note that this operation is intended for testing/debugging purposes only. It only supports stack data items that are one of C++'s predefined data types (`int`, `char`, and so forth).

Laboratory 5: Cover Sheet

Name _____ Date _____

Section _____

Place a check mark in the *Assigned* column next to the exercises your instructor has assigned to you. Attach this cover sheet to the front of the packet of materials you submit following the laboratory.

Activities	Assigned: Check or list exercise numbers	Completed
Prelab Exercise		
Bridge Exercise		
In-lab Exercise 1		
In-lab Exercise 2		
In-lab Exercise 3		
Postlab Exercise 1		
Postlab Exercise 2		
Total		

Laboratory 5: Prelab Exercise

Name _____ Date _____

Section _____

Multiple implementations of an ADT are necessary if the ADT is to perform efficiently in a variety of operating environments. Depending on the hardware and the application, you may want an implementation that reduces the execution time of some (or all) of the ADT operations, or you may want an implementation that reduces the amount of memory used to store the ADT data items. In this laboratory you will develop two implementations of the Stack ADT. One implementation stores the stack in an array, the other stores each data item separately and links the data items together to form a stack.

Step 1: Implement the operations in the Stack ADT using an array to store the stack data items. Stacks change in size; therefore, you need to store the maximum number of data items the stack can hold (maxSize) and the array index of the topmost data item in the stack (top), along with the stack data items themselves (dataItems). Base your implementation on the following declarations from the file *stackarr.h*. An implementation of the showStructure operation is given in the file *show5.cpp*.

```
const int defMaxStackSize = 10;    // Default maximum stack size

template < class DT >
class Stack
{
  public:

    // Constructor
    Stack ( int maxNumber = defMaxStackSize ) throw ( bad_alloc );

    // Destructor
    ~Stack ();

    // Stack manipulation operations
    void push ( const DT &newDataItem )     // Push data item
        throw ( logic_error );
    DT pop ()                               // Pop data item
        throw ( logic_error );
    void clear ();                          // Clear stack

    // Stack status operations
    bool isEmpty () const;                  // Stack is empty
    bool isFull () const;                   // Stack is full

    // Output the stack structure – used in testing/debugging
    void showStructure () const;
```

```
    private:

        // Data members
        int maxSize,     // Maximum number of data items in the stack
            top;         // Index of the top data item
        DT *dataItems;   // Array containing the stack data items
};
```

Step 2: Save your array implementation of the Stack ADT in the file *stackarr.cpp*. Be sure to document your code.

In your array implementation of the Stack ADT, you allocate the memory used to store a stack when the stack is declared (constructed). The resulting array must be large enough to hold the largest stack you might possibly need in a particular application. Unfortunately, most of the time the stack will not actually be this large and the extra memory will go unused.

An alternative approach is to allocate memory data item by data item as new data items are added to the stack. In this way, you allocate memory only when you actually need it. Because memory is allocated over time, however, the data items do not occupy a contiguous set of memory locations. As a result, you need to link the data items together to form a linked list representation of a stack, as shown in the following figure.

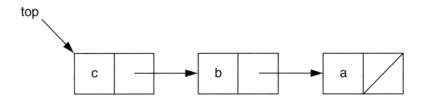

Creating a linked list implementation of the Stack ADT presents a somewhat more challenging programming task than did developing an array implementation. One way to simplify this task is to divide the implementation into two templated classes: one focusing on the overall stack structure (the Stack class) and another focusing on the individual nodes in the linked list (the StackNode class).

Let's begin with the StackNode class. Each node in the linked list contains a stack data item and a pointer to the node containing the next data item in the list. The only function provided by the StackNode class is a constructor that creates a specified node.

Access to the StackNode class is restricted to member functions of the Stack class. Other classes are blocked from referencing linked list nodes directly by declaring all the members of StackNode to be private. The members of StackNode are made accessible to the Stack class by declaring Stack to be a **friend** of StackNode. These properties are reflected in the following class declaration from the file *stacklnk.h.*

```
template < class DT >       // Forward declaration of the Stack class
class Stack;

template < class DT >
class StackNode             // Facilitator class for the Stack class
{
    private:
```

```
    // Constructor
    StackNode ( const DT &nodeData, StackNode *nextPtr );

    // Data members
    DT dataItem;            // Stack data item
    StackNode *next;        // Pointer to the next data item

  friend class Stack<DT>;
};
```

Notice the first two lines in the StackNode declaration above. The forward declaration is how C++ solves a classic compiler dilemma. StackNode makes reference to Stack in the statement

```
friend class Stack<DT>;
```

but the compiler has not yet encountered Stack and would normally issue an error message about referencing an unknown data type. We could move the declaration of Stack up above that of StackNode, thus ensuring that the compiler would have already seen Stack before it is referenced in StackNode. The problem that arises then is that the declaration of Stack contains a reference to StackNode before StackNode is declared. This is a catch-22, because they can't both occur first in the program.

C++ solves this problem by allowing the existence of a data type to be announced before it is actually declared. The compiler notes that it will be declared later and continues. This is similar to the introduction of a function prototype at the beginning of a program, well before the function definition is encountered.

The StackNode class constructor is used to add nodes to the stack. The following statement, for example, adds a node containing 'd' to a stack of characters. Note that template parameter DT must be equivalent to type char and top is of type StackNode*.

```
top = new StackNode<DT>('d',top);
```

The new operator allocates memory for a linked list node and calls the StackNode constructor passing both the data item to be inserted ('d') and a pointer to next node in the list (top).

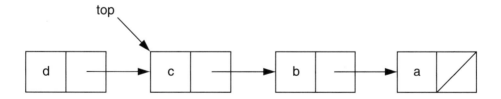

Finally, the assignment operator assigns a pointer to the newly allocated node to top, thereby completing the creation and linking of the node.

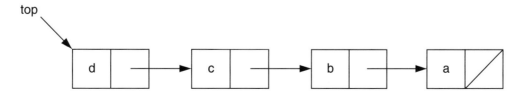

The member functions of the `Stack` class implement the operations in the Stack ADT. A pointer is maintained to the node at the beginning of the linked list or, equivalently, the top of the stack. The following declaration for the `Stack` class is given in the file *stacklnk.h.*

```
template < class DT >
class Stack
{
  public:

    // Constructor
    Stack ( int ignored = 0 );

    // Destructor
    ~Stack ();

    // Stack manipulation operations
    void push ( const DT &newDataItem )    // Push data item
        throw ( bad_alloc );
    DT pop ()                              // Pop data item
        throw ( logic_error );
    void clear ();                         // Clear stack

    // Stack status operations
    bool isEmpty () const;                 // Is stack empty?
    bool isFull () const;                  // Is stack full?

    // Output the stack structure — used in testing/debugging
    void showStructure () const;

  private:

    // Data member
    StackNode<DT> *top;                    // Pointer to the top data item
};
```

Step 3: Implement the operations in the Stack ADT using a singly linked list to store the stack data items. Each node in the linked list should contain a stack data item (`dataItem`) and a pointer to the node containing the next data item in the stack (`next`). Your implementation also should maintain a pointer to the node containing the topmost data item in the stack (`top`). Base your implementation on the class declarations in the file *stacklnk.h.* An implementation of the `showStructure` operation is given in the file *show5.cpp.*

Step 4: Save your linked list implementation of the Stack ADT in the file *stacklnk.cpp.* Be sure to document your code.

Laboratory 5: Bridge Exercise

Name _____ Date _____

Section _____

Check with your instructor whether you are to complete this exercise prior to your lab period or during lab.

The test program in the file *test5.cpp* allows you to interactively test your implementation of the Stack ADT using the following commands.

Command	Action
+x	Push data item x onto the top of the stack.
-	Pop the top data item and output it.
E	Report whether the stack is empty.
F	Report whether the stack is full.
C	Clear the stack.
Q	Exit the test program.

Step 1: Compile and link the test program. Note that compiling this program will compile your array implementation of the Stack ADT (in the file *stackarr.cpp*) to produce an array implementation for a stack of characters.

Step 2: Complete the following test plan by adding test cases in which you

- Pop a data item from a stack containing only one data item
- Push a data item onto a stack that has been emptied by a series of pops
- Pop a data item from a full stack (array implementation)
- Clear the stack

Step 3: Execute your test plan. If you discover mistakes in your array implementation of the Stack ADT, correct them and execute your test plan again.

Step 4: Modify the test program so that your linked list implementation of the Stack ADT in the file *stacklnk.cpp* is included in place of your array implementation.

Step 5: Recompile and relink the test program. Note that recompiling this program will compile your linked list implementation of the Stack ADT (in the file *stacklnk.cpp*) to produce a linked list implementation for a stack of characters.

Step 6: Use your test plan to check your linked list implementation of the Stack ADT. If you discover mistakes in your implementation, correct them and execute your test plan again.

Test Plan for the Operations in the Stack ADT

Test Case	Commands	Expected Result	Checked
Series of pushes	+a +b +c +d	a b c **d**	
Series of pops	- - -	**a**	
More pushes	+e +f	a e **f**	
More pops	- -	**a**	
Empty? Full?	E F	False False	
Empty the stack	-	Empty stack	
Empty? Full?	E F	True False	

Note: The topmost data item is shown in **bold**.

Laboratory 5: In-lab Exercise 1

Name _____ Date _____

Section _____

We commonly write arithmetic expressions in **infix form**, that is, with each operator placed between its operands, as in the following expression:

$$(3 + 4) * (5 / 2)$$

Although we are comfortable writing expressions in this form, infix form has the disadvantage that parentheses must be used to indicate the order in which operators are to be evaluated. These parentheses, in turn, greatly complicate the evaluation process.

Evaluation is much easier if we can simply evaluate operators from left to right. Unfortunately, this evaluation strategy will not work with the infix form of arithmetic expressions. However, it will work if the expression is in **postfix form**. In the postfix form of an arithmetic expression, each operator is placed immediately after its operands. The expression above is written in postfix form as

$$3 4 + 5 2 / *$$

Note that both forms place the numbers in the same order (reading from left to right). The order of the operators is different, however, because the operators in the postfix form are positioned in the order in which they are evaluated. The resulting postfix expression is hard to read at first, but it is easy to evaluate. All you need is a stack on which to place intermediate results.

Suppose you have an arithmetic expression in postfix form that consists of a sequence of single-digit, nonnegative integers and the four basic arithmetic operators (addition, subtraction, multiplication, and division). This expression can be evaluated using the following algorithm in conjunction with a stack of floating-point numbers.

Read in the expression character by character. As each character is read in:

- If the character corresponds to a single-digit number (characters '0' to '9'), then push the corresponding floating-point number onto the stack.
- If the character corresponds to one of the arithmetic operators (characters '+', '-', '*', and '/'), then
- Pop a number off of the stack. Call it *operand1*.
- Pop a number off of the stack. Call it *operand2*.
- Combine these operands using the arithmetic operator, as follows:
  Result = operand2 operator operand1
- Push *result* onto the stack.
- When the end of the expression is reached, pop the remaining number off the stack. This number is the value of the expression.

Applying this algorithm to the arithmetic expression

$$3 4 + 5 2 / *$$

yields the following computation

'3'   : Push 3.0

'4'   : Push 4.0

'+'   : Pop, *operand1* = 4.0

          Pop, *operand2* = 3.0

          Combine, *result* = 3.0 + 4.0 = 7.0

          Push 7.0

'5'   : Push 5.0

'2'   : Push 2.0

'/'   : Pop, *operand1* = 2.0

          Pop, *operand2* = 5.0

          Combine, *result* = 5.0 / 2.0 = 2.5

          Push 2.5

'*'   : Pop, *operand1* = 2.5

          Pop, *operand2* = 7.0

          Combine, *result* = 7.0 * 2.5 = 17.5

          Push 17.5

'\n'   : Pop, Value of expression = 17.5

Step 1: Create a program that reads the postfix form of an arithmetic expression, evaluates it, and outputs the result. Assume that the expression consists of single-digit, nonnegative integers ('0' to '9') and the four basic arithmetic operators ('+', '−', '*', and '/'). Further assume that the arithmetic expression is input from the keyboard with all the characters on one line. Save your program in a file called *postfix.cpp*.

Step 2: Complete the following test plan by filling in the expected result for each arithmetic expression. You may wish to include additional arithmetic expressions in this test plan.

Step 3: Execute the test plan. If you discover mistakes in your program, correct them and execute the test plan again.

Test Plan for the Postfix Arithmetic Expression Evaluation Program

Test Case	Arithmetic Expression	Expected Result	Checked
One operator	34+		
Nested operators	34+52/*		
Uneven nesting	93*2+1-		
All operators at end	4675-+*		
Zero dividend	02/		
Single-digit number	7		

Laboratory 5: In-lab Exercise 2

Name _____   Date _____

Section _____

Rather than have the array implementation of a stack grow upward from array entry 0 toward entry maxSize−1, you can just as easily construct an implementation that begins at array entry maxSize−1 and grows downward toward entry 0. You could then combine this "downward" array implementation with the "upward" array implementation you created in the Prelab to form an implementation of a Double Stack ADT in which a pair of stacks occupy the same array—assuming that the total number of data items in *both* stacks never exceeds maxSize.

   If this appears to be a strange type of double stack, it is not one that we have made up. It is a classic approach to managing part of a process's memory in operating systems.

Step 1:   Create an implementation of the Stack ADT using an array in which the stack grows downward. Base your implementation on the declarations in the file *stackdwn.h* (these are identical to the declarations in the file *stackarr.h*). An implementation of the showStructure operation is given in the file *show5.cpp*.

Step 2:   Save your "downward" array implementation of the Stack ADT in the file *stackdwn.cpp*.

Step 3:   Modify the test program *test5.cpp* so that your "downward" array implementation of the Stack ADT in the file *stackdwn.cpp* is included in place of your "upward" array implementation.

Step 4:   Use the test plan you created in In-lab Exercise 1 to check your "downward" array implementation of the Stack ADT. If you discover mistakes in your implementation, correct them and execute your test plan again.

Laboratory 5: In-lab Exercise 3

Name _____ Date _____

Section _____

One of the tasks that compilers and interpreters must frequently perform is deciding whether some pairs of expression delimiters are properly paired, even if they are embedded multiple pairs deep. Consider the following C++ expression.

```
a = (f[b] - (c+d)) / 2;
```

The compiler has to be able to determine which pairs of opening and closing delimiters—parentheses, square braces, etc.—go together and whether the whole expression is correctly delimited. A number of possible errors can occur because of unpaired delimiters or because of improperly placed delimiters. For instance, the expression below lacks a closing parenthesis.

```
a = (f[b] - (c+d) / 2;
```

The following expression is also invalid. There are the correct numbers of parenthesis and braces, but they are not correctly balanced. The first closing parenthesis does not match the most recent opening delimiter, a brace.

```
a = (f[b) - (c+d]) / 2;
```

A stack is extremely helpful in implementing solutions to this type of problem because of its LIFO—Last In, First Out—behavior. A closing delimiter must correctly match the most recently encountered opening delimiter. This is handled by pushing opening delimiters onto a stack as they are encountered. When a closing delimiter is encountered, it should be possible to pop the matching opening delimiter off the stack. If it is determined that every closing delimiter had a matching opening delimiter, then the expression is valid.

```
bool delimitersOk( const string &expression )
```

Requirements:
None

Results:
Returns `true` if all the parentheses and braces in the string are legally paired. Otherwise, returns `false`.

Step 1: Save a copy of the file *delim.cs* as *delim.cpp*. Implement the delimitersOk operation inside the *delim.cpp* program file.

Step 2: Complete the following test plan by adding test cases that check whether your implementation of the delimitersOk operation correctly detects improperly paired delimiters in input expressions. Note that it is not required that the input be valid C++ expressions, just that the delimiters are properly used.

Step 3: Execute your test plan. If you discover mistakes in your implementation of the delimitersOk function, correct them and execute the test plan again.

Test Plan for the delimitersOk operation

Test Case	Commands	Expected Result	Checked
Valid expression with parentheses	`3 * (a+b)`	`true`	
Valid expression with mixed delimiters	`f[3 * (a+b)]`	`true`	
Invalid expression with mixed delimiters	`(f[b)-(c+d])/2;`	`false`	
Empty expression	*Empty string<Newline>*	`true`	
Improperly paired brace	`a = f[b + 3`		

Note: The improperly matched delimiters are shown in **bold**.

Laboratory 5: Postlab Exercise 1

Name _____ Date _____

Section _____

Given the input string "abc", which of the permutations of this string listed in part A can be output by a code fragment consisting of only the statement pairs

```
cin >> ch;    permuteStack.push(ch);
```

and

```
ch = permuteStack.pop();    cout << ch;
```

where `ch` is a character and `permuteStack` is a stack of characters? Note that each of the statement pairs may be repeated several times within the code fragment and that the statement pairs may be in any order. For instance, the code fragment

```
cin >> ch;    permuteStack.push(ch);
cin >> ch;    permuteStack.push(ch);
cin >> ch;    permuteStack.push(ch);
ch = permuteStack.pop();    cout << ch;
ch = permuteStack.pop();    cout << ch;
ch = permuteStack.pop();    cout << ch;
```

outputs the string "cba".

Part A

For each of the permutations listed below, give a code fragment that outputs the permutation or a brief explanation of why the permutation cannot be produced.

"abc"   "acb"

"bac"   "bca"

"cab"   "cba"

Part B

Given the input string "abcd", which four-character permutations beginning with the character 'd' can be output by a code fragment of the form described above? Why can only these permutations be produced?

Laboratory 5: Postlab Exercise 2

Name _____   Date _____

Section _____

In In-lab Exercise 1, you used a stack to evaluate arithmetic expressions. Describe another application where you might use the Stack ADT. What type of information does your application store in each stack data item?

Queue ADT

In this laboratory you will

- Create two implementations of the Queue ADT—one based on an array representation of a queue, the other based on a singly linked list representation

- Create a program that simulates the flow of customers through a line

- Create an array implementation of a dequeue

- Analyze the memory requirements of your array and linked list queue representations

Objectives

Overview

This laboratory focuses on another constrained linear data structure, the **queue**. The data items in a queue are ordered from least recently added (the **front**) to most recently added (the **rear**). Insertions are performed at the rear of the queue and deletions are performed at the front. You use the **enqueue** operation to insert data items and the **dequeue** operation to remove data items. A sequence of enqueues and dequeues is shown below.

Enqueue a	*Enqueue b*	*Enqueue c*	*Dequeue*	*Dequeue*
a	a b	a b c	b c	c
←front	←front	←front	←front	←front

The movement of data items through a queue reflects the "first in, first out" (FIFO) behavior that is characteristic of the flow of customers in a line or the transmission of information across a data channel. Queues are routinely used to regulate the flow of physical objects, information, and requests for resources (or services) through a system. Operating systems, for example, use queues to control access to system resources such as printers, files, and communications lines. Queues also are widely used in simulations to model the flow of objects or information through a system.

Queue ADT

Data Items

The data items in a queue are of generic type DT.

Structure

The queue data items are linearly ordered from least recently added (the front) to most recently added (the rear). Data items are inserted at the rear of the queue (enqueued) and are removed from the front of the queue (dequeued).

Operations

```
Queue ( int maxNumber = defMaxQueueSize ) throw ( bad_alloc )
```

Requirements:
None

Results:
Constructor. Creates an empty queue. Allocates enough memory for a queue containing `maxNumber` data items (if necessary).

```
~Queue ()
```

Requirements:
None

Results:
Destructor. Deallocates (frees) the memory used to store a queue.

```
void enqueue ( const DT &newDataItem ) throw ( logic_error )
```

Requirements:
Queue is not full.

Results:
Inserts `newDataItem` at the rear of a queue.

```
DT dequeue () throw ( logic_error )
```

Requirements:
Queue is not empty.

Results:
Removes the least recently added (front) data item from a queue and returns it.

```
void clear ()
```

Requirements:
None

Results:
Removes all the data items in a queue.

```
bool isEmpty () const
```

Requirements:
None

Results:
Returns `true` if a queue is empty. Otherwise, returns `false`.

```
bool isFull () const
```

Requirements:
None

Results:
Returns `true` if a queue is full. Otherwise, returns `false`.

```
void showStructure () const
```

Requirements:
None

Results:
Outputs the data items in a queue. If the queue is empty, outputs "Empty queue". Note that this operation is intended for testing/debugging purposes only. It only supports queue data items that are one of C++'s predefined data types (`int`, `char`, and so forth).

Laboratory 6: Cover Sheet

Name _____ Date _____

Section _____

Place a check mark in the *Assigned* column next to the exercises your instructor has assigned to you. Attach this cover sheet to the front of the packet of materials you submit following the laboratory.

Activities	Assigned: Check or list exercise numbers	Completed
Prelab Exercise		
Bridge Exercise		
In-lab Exercise 1		
In-lab Exercise 2		
In-lab Exercise 3		
Postlab Exercise 1		
Postlab Exercise 2		
Total		

Laboratory 6: Prelab Exercise

Name _____ Date _____

Section _____

In this laboratory you will create two implementations of the Queue ADT. One of these implementations is based on an array; the other is based on a singly linked list. Following the example introduced in Lab 5, the generic data type will be named DT for Data Type.

Step 1: Implement the operations in the Queue ADT using an array to store the queue data items. Queues change in size; therefore, you need to store the maximum number of data items the queue can hold (maxSize) and the array index of the data items at the front and rear of the queue (front and rear), along with the queue data items themselves (dataItems). Base your implementation on the following declarations from the file *queuearr.h*. An implementation of the showStructure operation is given in the file *show6.cpp*.

```cpp
const int defMaxQueueSize = 10;   // Default maximum queue size

template < class DT >
class Queue
{
  public:

    // Constructor
    Queue ( int maxNumber = defMaxQueueSize ) throw ( bad_alloc );

    // Destructor
    ~Queue ();

    // Queue manipulation operations
    void enqueue ( const DT &newData )      // Enqueue data item
        throw ( logic_error );
    DT dequeue ()                           // Dequeue data item
        throw ( logic_error );
    void clear ();                          // Clear queue

    // Queue status operations
    bool isEmpty () const;                  // Queue is empty
    bool isFull () const;                   // Queue is full

    // Output the queue structure — used in testing/debugging
    void showStructure () const;
```

```
   private:

      // Data members
      int maxSize,    // Maximum number of data data items in the queue
          front,      // Index of the front data data item
          rear;       // Index of the rear data data item
      DT *dataItems;  // Array containing the queue data items
};
```

Step 2: Save your array implementation of the Queue ADT in the file *queuearr.cpp*. Be sure to document your code.

Step 3: Implement the operations in the Queue ADT using a singly linked list to store the queue data items. Each node in the linked list should contain a queue data item (`dataItem`) and a pointer to the node containing the next data item in the queue (`next`). Your implementation also should maintain pointers to the nodes containing the front and rear data items in the queue (`front` and `rear`). Base your implementation on the following declarations from the file *queuelnk.h*. An implementation of the `showStructure` operation is given in the file *show6.cpp*.

```
template < class DT >           // Forward declaration of the Queue class
class Queue;

template < class DT >
class QueueNode                 // Facilitator class for the Queue class
{
  private:

     // Constructor
     QueueNode ( const DT &nodeData, QueueNode *nextPtr );

     // Data members
     DT dataItem;             // Queue data item
     QueueNode *next;         // Pointer to the next data item

  friend class Queue<DT>;
};

template < class DT >
class Queue
{
  public:

     // Constructor
     Queue ( int ignored = 0 );

     // Destructor
     ~Queue ();

     // Queue manipulation operations
     void enqueue ( const DT &newData )           // Enqueue data data item
         throw ( logic_error );
```

```
    DT dequeue ()                          // Dequeue data data item
        throw ( logic_error );

    void clear ();                         // Clear queue

    // Queue status operations
    bool isEmpty () const;                 // Queue is empty
    bool isFull () const;                  // Queue is full

    // Output the queue structure — used in testing/debugging
    void showStructure () const;

  private:

    // Data members
    QueueNode<DT> *front,    // Pointer to the front node
                  *rear;     // Pointer to the rear node
};
```

Step 4: Save your linked list implementation of the Queue ADT in the file *queuelnk.cpp.* Be sure to document your code.

Laboratory 6: Bridge Exercise

Name _____ Date _____

Section _____

Check with your instructor whether you are to complete this exercise prior to your lab period or during lab.

The test program in the file *test6.cpp* allows you to interactively test your implementations of the Queue ADT using the following commands.

Command	Action
+x	Enqueue data item x.
-	Dequeue a data item and output it.
E	Report whether the queue is empty.
F	Report whether the queue is full.
C	Clear the queue.
Q	Exit the test program.

Step 1: Compile and link the test program. Note that compiling this program will compile your array implementation of the Queue ADT (in the file *queuearr.cpp*) to produce an array implementation for a queue of characters.

Step 2: Complete the following test plan by adding test cases in which you

- Enqueue a data item onto a queue that has been emptied by a series of dequeues
- Combine enqueues and dequeues so that you "go around the end" of the array (array implementation)
- Dequeue a data item from a full queue (array implementation)
- Clear the queue

Step 3: Execute your test plan. If you discover mistakes in your array implementation of the Queue ADT, correct them and execute your test plan again.

Step 4: Modify the test program so that your linked list implementation of the Queue ADT in the file *queuelnk.cpp* is included in place of your array implementation.

Step 5: Recompile and relink the test program. Note that recompiling this program will compile your linked list implementation of the Queue ADT (in the file *queuelnk.cpp*) to produce a linked list implementation for a queue of characters.

Step 6: Use your test plan to check your linked list implementation of the Queue ADT. If you discover mistakes in your implementation, correct them and execute your test plan again.

Test Plan for the Operations in the Queue ADT

Test Case	Commands	Expected Result	Checked
Series of enqueues	+a +b +c +d	**a** b c d	
Series of dequeues	- - -	**d**	
More enqueues	+e +f	**d** e f	
More dequeues	- -	**f**	
Empty? Full?	E F	False False	
Empty the queue	-	Empty queue	
Empty? Full?	E F	True False	

Note: The front data item is shown in **bold**.

Laboratory 6: In-lab Exercise 1

Name _____ Date _____

Section _____

In this exercise you will use a queue to simulate the flow of customers through a check-out line in a store. In order to create this simulation, you must model both the passage of time and the flow of customers through the line. You can model time using a loop in which each pass corresponds to a set time interval—1 minute, for example. You can model the flow of customers using a queue in which each data item corresponds to a customer in the line.

In order to complete the simulation, you need to know the rate at which customers join the line, as well as the rate at which they are served and leave the line. Suppose the check-out line has the following properties:

- One customer is served and leaves the line every minute (assuming there is at least one customer waiting to be served during that minute).
- Between zero and two customers join the line every minute, where there is a 50% chance that no customers arrive, a 25% chance that one customer arrives, and a 25% chance that two customers arrive.

You can simulate the flow of customers through the line during a time period n minutes long using the following algorithm.

Initialize the queue to empty.

for (minute = 0 ; minute < n ; ++minute)
{

    If the queue is not empty, then remove the customer at the front of the queue.

    Compute a random number k between 0 and 3.

    If k is 1, then add one customer to the line. If k is 2, then add two customers
      to the line. Otherwise (if k is 0 or 3), do not add any customers to the line.

}

Calling the rand() function is a simple way to generate pseudo-random numbers. It should be available through the <cstdlib> function set. Generating random numbers does vary from platform to platform because of compiler and operating system differences. You may need to get help from your lab instructor on how to generate random numbers in your particular context.

Step 1: Using the program shell given in the file *storesim.cs* as a basis, create a program that uses the Queue ADT to implement the model described in the preceding paragraphs. Your program should update the following information during each simulated minute; that is, during each pass through the loop:

- The total number of customers served
- The combined length of time these customers spent waiting in line
- The maximum length of time any of these customers spent waiting in line

To compute how long a customer waited to be served, you need to store the "minute" that the customer was added to the queue as part of the queue data item corresponding to that customer.

Step 2: Use your program to simulate the flow of customers through the line and complete the following table. Note that the average wait is the combined waiting time divided by the total number of customers served.

Time (minutes)	Total Number of Customers Served	Average Wait	Longest Wait
30			
60			
120			
480			

Laboratory 6: In-lab Exercise 2

Name _____ Date _____

Section _____

A **deque** (or double-ended queue) is a linear data structure that allows data items to be inserted and removed at both ends. Adding the operations described below will transform your Queue ADT into a Deque ADT.

```
void putFront ( const DT &newDataItem ) throw ( logic_error )
```

Requirements:
Queue is not full.

Results:
Inserts newDataItem at the front of a queue. The order of the preexisting data items is left unchanged.

```
DT getRear () throw ( logic_error )
```

Requirements:
Queue is not empty.

Results:
Removes the most recently added (rear) data item from a queue and returns it. The remainder of the queue is left unchanged.

Step 1: Implement these operations using the array representation of a queue and add them to the file *queuearr.cpp*. Prototypes for these operations are included in the declaration of the Queue class in the file *queuearr.h*.

Step 2: Activate the '>' (put in front) and '=' (get from rear) commands in the test program *test6.cpp* by removing the comment delimiter (and the character '>' or '=') from the lines that begin with "//>" and "//=".

Step 3: Complete the following test plan by adding test cases in which you

- Insert a data item at the front of a newly emptied queue
- Remove a data item from the rear of a queue containing only one data item
- "Go around the end" of the array using each of these operations
- Mix putFront and getRear with enqueue and dequeue

Step 4: Execute your test plan. If you discover mistakes in your implementation of these operations, correct them and execute the test plan again.

Test Plan for the `putFront` and `getRear` operations

Test Case	Commands	Expected Result	Checked
Series of calls to putFront	>a >b >c >d	**d** c b a	
Series of calls to getRear	= = =	**d**	
More calls to putFront	>e >f	**f** e d	
More calls to getRear	= =	**f**	

Note: The front data item is shown in **bold**.

Laboratory 6: In-lab Exercise 3

Name _____   Date _____

Section _____

When a queue is used as part of a model or simulation, the modeler is often very interested in how many data items are on the queue at various points in time. This statistic is produced by the following operation.

```
int getLength () const
```

Requirements:
None

Results:
Returns the number of data items in a queue.

Step 1: Create an implementation of this operation using the array representation of a queue and add it to the file *queuearr.cpp*. A prototype for this operation is included in the declaration of the Queue class in the file *queuearr.h*.

Step 2: Activate the '#' (length) command in the test program *test6.cpp* by removing the comment delimiter (and the character '#') from the lines that begin with "//#".

Step 3: Complete the following test plan by adding test cases in which you check the length of empty queues and queues that "go around the end" of the array.

Step 4: Execute your test plan. If you discover mistakes in your implementation of the length operation, correct them and execute the test plan again.

Test Plan for the `length` Operation

Test Case	Commands	Expected Result	Checked
Series of enqueues	+a +b +c +d	a b c d	
Length	#	4	
Series of dequeues	- - -	d	
Length	#	1	
More enqueues	+e +f	d e f	
Length	#	3	

Note: The front data item is shown in **bold**.

Laboratory 6: Postlab Exercise 1

Name _____ Date _____

Section _____

Part A

Given the following memory requirements and a queue containing one hundred integers, compare the amount of memory used by your array representation of the queue with the amount of memory used by your singly linked list representation. Assume that the array representation allows a queue to contain a maximum of one hundred data items.

Integer   2 bytes

Address (pointer)   4 bytes

Note: Integer and pointer memory requirements vary depending on the operating system and compiler. Integers and addresses range in size from 1 to 8 bytes, or larger. The values above represent a specific platform and were chosen for simplicity of calculation.

Part B

Suppose that you have ten queues of integers. Of these ten queues, four are 50% full, and the remaining six are 10% full. Compare the amount of memory used by your array representation of these queues with the amount of memory used by your singly linked list representation. Assume that the array representation allows a queue to contain a maximum of one hundred data items.

Laboratory 6: Postlab Exercise 2

Name _____ Date _____

Section _____

In In-lab Exercise 1, you used a queue to simulate the flow of customers through a line. Describe another application where you might use the Queue ADT. What type of information does your application store in each queue data item?

Singly Linked List Implementation of the List ADT

Objectives

In this laboratory you will:

■ Implement the List ADT using a singly linked list

■ Create a program that displays a slide show

■ Examine how a fresh perspective on insertion and deletion can produce more efficient linked list implementations of these operations

■ Analyze the efficiency of your singly linked list implementation of the List ADT

Overview

In Laboratory 3 you created an implementation of the List ADT using an array to store the list data items. Although this approach is intuitive, it is not terribly efficient either in terms of memory usage or time. It wastes memory by allocating an array that is large enough to store what you estimate to be the maximum number of data items a list will ever hold. In most cases, the list is rarely this large and the extra memory simply goes unused. In addition, the insertion and deletion operations require shifting data items back and forth within the array, a very time-consuming task.

In this laboratory, you implement the List ADT using a singly linked list. This implementation allocates memory data item by data item as data items are added to the list. Equally important, a linked list can be reconfigured following an insertion or deletion simply by changing one or two links.

List ADT

Data Items

The data items in a list are of generic type DT.

Structure

The data items form a linear structure in which list data items follow one after the other, from the beginning of the list to its end. The ordering of the data items is determined by when and where each data item is inserted into the list and is *not* a function of the data contained in the list data items. At any point in time, one data item in any nonempty list is marked using the list's cursor. You travel through the list using operations that change the position of the cursor.

Operations

```
List ( int ignored = 0 )
```

Requirements:
None

Results:
Constructor. Creates an empty list. The argument is provided for call compatibility with the array implementation and is ignored.

```
~List ()
```

Requirements:
None

Results:
Destructor. Deallocates (frees) the memory used to store a list.

```
void insert ( const DT &newDataItem ) throw ( bad_alloc )
```

Requirements:
List is not full.

Results:
Inserts newDataItem into a list. If the list is not empty, then inserts newDataItem after the cursor. Otherwise, inserts newDataItem as the first (and only) data item in the list. In either case, moves the cursor to newDataItem.

```
void remove () throw ( logic_error )
```

Requirements:
List is not empty.

Results:
Removes the data item marked by the cursor from a list. If the resulting list is not empty, then moves the cursor to the data item that followed the deleted data item. If the deleted data item was at the end of the list, then moves the cursor to the beginning of the list.

```
void replace ( const DT &newDataItem ) throw ( logic_error )
```

Requirements:
List is not empty.

Results:
Replaces the data item marked by the cursor with `newDataItem`. The cursor remains at `newDataItem`.

```
void clear ()
```

Requirements:
None

Results:
Removes all the data items in a list.

```
bool isEmpty () const
```

Requirements:
None

Results:
Returns `true` if a list is empty. Otherwise, returns `false`.

```
bool isFull () const
```

Requirements:
None

Results:
Returns `true` if a list is full. Otherwise, returns `false`.

```
void gotoBeginning () throw ( logic_error )
```

Requirements:
List is not empty.

Results:
Moves the cursor to the beginning of the list.

```
void gotoEnd () throw ( logic_error )
```

Requirements:
List is not empty.

Results:
Moves the cursor to the end of the list.

```
bool gotoNext () throw ( logic_error )
```

Requirements:
List is not empty.

Results:
If the cursor is not at the end of a list, then moves the cursor to mark the next data item in the list and returns `true`. Otherwise, returns `false`.

```
bool gotoPrior () throw ( logic_error )
```

Requirements:
List is not empty.

Results:
If the cursor is not at the beginning of a list, then moves the cursor to mark the preceding data item in the list and returns `true`. Otherwise, returns `false`.

```
DT getCursor () const throw ( logic_error )
```

Requirements:
List is not empty.

Results:
Returns a copy of the data item marked by the cursor.

```
void showStructure () const
```

Requirements:
None

Results:
Outputs the data items in a list. If the list is empty, outputs "Empty list". Note that this operation is intended for testing/debugging purposes only. It supports only list data items that are one of C++'s predefined data types (`int`, `char`, and so forth).

Laboratory 7: Cover Sheet

Name _____   Date _____

Section _____

Place a check mark in the *Assigned* column next to the exercises your instructor has assigned to you. Attach this cover sheet to the front of the packet of materials you submit following the laboratory.

Activities	Assigned: Check or list exercise numbers	Completed
Prelab Exercise		
Bridge Exercise		
In-lab Exercise 1		
In-lab Exercise 2		
In-lab Exercise 3		
Postlab Exercise 1		
Postlab Exercise 2		
Total		

Laboratory 7: Prelab Exercise

Name _____   Date _____

Section _____

Your linked list implementation of the List ADT uses a pair of classes, ListNode and List, to represent individual nodes and the overall list structure, respectively. If you are unfamiliar with this approach to linked lists, read the discussion in Laboratory 5.

Step 1: Implement the operations in the List ADT using a singly linked list. Each node in the linked list should contain a list data item (dataItem) and a pointer to the node containing the next data item in the list (next). Your implementation also should maintain pointers to the node at the beginning of the list (head) and the node containing the data item marked by the cursor (cursor). Base your implementation on the following declarations from the file *listlnk.h*. An implementation of the showStructure operation is given in the file *show7.cpp*.

```
template < class DT >          // Forward declaration of the List class
class List;

template < class DT >
class ListNode                 // Facilitator class for the List class
{
  private:

    // Constructor
    ListNode ( const DT &nodeData, ListNode *nextPtr );

    // Data members
    DT dataItem;       // List data item
    ListNode *next;    // Pointer to the next list node

  friend class List<DT>;
};

//---------------------—

template < class DT >
class List
{
  public:

    // Constructor
    List ( int ignored = 0 );

    // Destructor
    ~List ();

    // List manipulation operations
    void insert ( const DT &newData ) throw ( bad_alloc );    // Insert after cursor
```

```
    void remove () throw ( logic_error );              // Remove data item
    void replace ( const DT &newData ) throw ( logic_error ); // Replace data item
    void clear ();                                     // Clear list

    // List status operations
    bool isEmpty () const;                             // List is empty
    bool isFull () const;                              // List is full

    // List iteration operations
    void gotoBeginning () throw ( logic_error );       // Go to beginning
    void gotoEnd () throw ( logic_error );             // Go to end
    bool gotoNext () throw ( logic_error );            // Go to next data
                                                       //  item
    bool gotoPrior () throw ( logic_error );           // Go to prior item

    DT getCursor () const throw ( logic_error );       // Return item

    // Output the list structure — used in testing/debugging
    void showStructure () const;

  private:

    // Data members
    ListNode<DT> *head,       // Pointer to the beginning of the list
                 *cursor;     // Cursor pointer
};
```

Step 2: Save your implementation of the List ADT in the file *listlnk.cpp*. Be sure to document your code.

Laboratory 7: Bridge Exercise

Name _____ Date _____

Section _____

Check with your instructor whether you are to complete this exercise prior to your lab period or during lab.

The test program in the file *test7.cpp* allows you to interactively test your implementation of the List ADT using the following commands.

Command	Action
+x	Insert data item x after the cursor.
-	Remove the data item marked by the cursor.
=x	Replace the data item marked by the cursor with data item x.
@	Display the data item marked by the cursor.
N	Go to the next data item.
P	Go to the prior data item.
<	Go to the beginning of the list.
>	Go to the end of the list.
E	Report whether the list is empty.
F	Report whether the list is full.
C	Clear the list.
Q	Quit the test program.

Step 1: Compile and link the test program. Note that compiling this program will compile your linked list implementation of the List ADT (in the file *listlnk.cpp*) to produce an implementation for a list of characters.

Step 2: Complete the following test plan by adding test cases that check whether your implementation of the List ADT correctly determines whether a list is empty and correctly inserts data items into a newly emptied list.

Step 3: Execute your test plan. If you discover mistakes in your implementation of the List ADT, correct them and execute your test plan again.

Test Plan for the Operations in the List ADT

Test Case	Commands	Expected Result	Checked
Insert at end	+a +b +c +d	a b c **d**	
Travel from beginning	< N N	a b **c** d	
Travel from end	> P P	a **b** c d	
Delete middle data item	-	a **c** d	
Insert in middle	+e +f +f	a c e f **f** d	
Remove last data item	> -	**a** c e f f	
Remove first data item	< -	**c** e f f	
Display data item	@	Returns c	
Replace data item	=g	**g** e f f	
Clear the list	C	Empty list	

Note: The data item marked by the cursor is shown in **bold**.

Step 4: Change the list in the test program from a list of characters to a list of integers by replacing the declarations for testList and testDataItem with

```
List<int> testList(8);    // Test list
int testDataItem;         // List data item
```

Step 5: Recompile and relink the test program. Note that recompiling this program will compile your implementation of the List ADT to produce an implementation for a list of integers.

Step 6: Replace the character data ('a'-'g') in your test plan with integer values.

Step 7: Execute your revised test plan using the revised test program. If you discover mistakes in your implementation of the List ADT, correct them and execute your revised test plan again.

Laboratory 7: In-lab Exercise 1

Name _____ Date _____

Section _____

List data items need not be one of C++'s built-in types. The following declaration, for example,

```
List<Slide> slideShow;
```

represents a slide show presentation as a list of slides where each slide is an object in the Slide class outlined below.

```
const int slideHeight = 10,        // Slide dimensions
          slideWidth  = 36;

class Slide
{
  public:

    void read ( ifstream &inFile );      // Read slide from file
    void display () const;               // Display slide and pause

  private:

    char image [slideHeight] [slideWidth];  // Slide image
    int pause;                              // Seconds to pause after
                                            //  displaying slide
};
```

Step 1: Using the program shell given in the file *slideshw.cs* as a basis, create a program that reads a list of slides from a file and displays the resulting slide show from beginning to end. Your program should pause for the specified length of time after displaying each slide. It then should clear the screen (by scrolling, if necessary) before displaying the next slide.

Assume that the file containing the slide show consists of repetitions of the following slide descriptor:

Time
Row 1
Row 2
...
Row 10

where Time is the length of time to pause after displaying a slide (in seconds) and Rows 1–10 form a slide image (each row is thirty-six characters long).

Note that list data items of type Slide should not cause problems with the routines in your implementation of the List ADT with the exception of the showStructure operation. Inactivate this operation by commenting out the showStructure() function.

Step 2: Test your program using the slide show in the file *slides.dat.*

Test Plan for the Slide Show Program

Test Case	Checked
Slide show in the file *slides.dat*	

Laboratory 7: In-lab Exercise 2

Name _____   Date _____

Section _____

In many applications, the order of the data items in a list changes over time. Not only are new data items added and existing ones removed, but data items are repositioned within the list. The following List ADT operation moves a data item to the beginning of a list.

```
void moveToBeginning () throw ( logic_error )
```

Requirements:
List is not empty.

Results:
Removes the data item marked by the cursor from a list and reinserts the data item at the beginning of the list. Moves the cursor to the beginning of the list.

Step 1: Implement this operation and add it to the file *listlnk.cpp*. A prototype for this operation is included in the declaration of the List class in the file *listlnk.h*.

Step 2: Activate the 'M' (move) command in the test program in the file *test7.cpp* by removing the comment delimiter (and the character 'M') from the lines beginning with "//M".

Step 3: Complete the following test plan by adding test cases that check whether your implementation of the `moveToBeginning` operation correctly processes attempts to move the first data item in a list and also moves within a single-data item list.

Step 4: Execute your test plan. If you discover mistakes in your implementation of the `moveToBeginning` operation, correct them and execute your test plan again.

Test Plan for the `moveToBeginning` **Operation**

Test Case	Commands	Expected Result	Checked
Set up list	+a +b +c +d	a b c d	
Move last data item	M	**d** a b c	
Move second data item	N M	**a** d b c	
Move third data item	N N M	**b** a d c	

Note: The data item marked by the cursor is shown in **bold**.

Laboratory 7: In-lab Exercise 3

Name _____   Date _____

Section _____

Sometimes a more effective approach to a problem can be found by looking at the problem a little differently. Consider the following List ADT operation:

```
void insertBefore ( const DT &newDataItem ) throw ( logic_error )
```

Requirements:
List is not full.

Results:
Inserts `newDataItem` into a list. If the list is not empty, then inserts `newDataItem` immediately before the cursor. Otherwise, inserts `newDataItem` as the first (and only) data item in the list. In either case, moves the cursor to `newDataItem`.

You can implement this operation using a singly linked list in two very different ways. The obvious approach is to iterate through the list from its beginning until you reach the node immediately before the cursor and then to insert `newDataItem` between this node and the cursor. A more efficient approach is to copy the data item pointed to by the cursor into a new node, to insert this node after the cursor, and to place `newDataItem` in the node pointed to by the cursor. This approach is more efficient because it does not require you to iterate through the list searching for the data item immediately before the cursor.

Step 1: Implement the `insertBefore` operation using the second (more efficient) approach and add it to the file *listlnk.cpp.* A prototype for this operation is included in the declaration of the List class in the file *listlnk.h.*

Step 2: Activate the '#' (insert before) command in the test program in the file *test7.cpp* by removing the comment delimiter (and the character '#') from the lines beginning with "//#".

Step 3: Complete the following test plan by adding test cases that check whether your implementation of the `insertBefore` operation correctly handles insertions into single data item lists and empty lists.

Step 4: Execute your test plan. If you discover mistakes in your implementation of the `insertBefore` operation, correct them and execute your test plan again.

Test Plan for the `insertBefore` **Operation**

Test Case	Commands	Expected Result	Checked
Set up list	+a +b +c	a b **c**	
Insert in middle	#d	a b **d** c	
Cascade inserts	#e	a b **e** d c	
Insert after head	P #f	a **f** b e d c	
Insert as head	P #g	**g** a f b e c	

Note: The data item marked by the cursor is shown in **bold**.

Laboratory 7: Postlab Exercise 1

Name _____ Date _____

Section _____

Given a list containing N data items, develop worst-case, order-of-magnitude estimates of the execution time of the following List ADT operations, assuming they are implemented using a linked list. Briefly explain your reasoning behind each estimate.

insert   O(   )

Explanation:

remove   O(   )

Explanation:

gotoNext   O(   )

Explanation:

gotoPrior   O(   )

Explanation:

Laboratory 7: Postlab Exercise 2

Name _____ Date _____

Section _____

Part A

In-lab Exercise 3 introduces a pair of approaches for implementing an `insertBefore` operation. One approach is straightforward, whereas the other is somewhat less obvious but more efficient. Describe how you might apply the latter approach to the `remove` operation. Use a diagram to illustrate your answer.

Part B

The resulting implementation of the `remove` operation has a worst-case, order of magnitude performance estimate of O(N). Does this estimate accurately reflect the performance of this implementation? Explain why or why not.

Copying and Comparing ADTs

Objectives

In this laboratory you will:

- Analyze the limitations of the default copy constructor, assignment operator, and equality operator

- Develop and implement an improved copy constructor, assignment operator, and equality operator for the singly linked implementation of the List ADT

- Learn about and implement a convert constructor

- Learn how to use the object's pointer `this` to improve function behavior

Overview

Whenever a variable is passed to a function using call by value, the compiler makes a copy of the variable. The function then manipulates this copy rather than the original argument. Once the function terminates, the copy is deleted.

How does the compiler know how to construct a copy of a particular argument? For C++'s predefined types, this task is straightforward. The compiler simply makes a **bitwise** (bit-by-bit) copy of the argument. Unfortunately, this approach does not work well with instances of classes such as the singly linked list that contain dynamically allocated data. Consider what happens when the call

```
dummy(testList);
```

is made to the following function:

```
void dummy ( List<DT> valueList );
```

A bitwise copy of list `testList` to list `valueList` copies pointers `testList.head` and `testList.cursor` to pointers `valueList.head` and `valueList.cursor`. The linked list of data items pointed to by `testList.head` is not copied and there are now two pointers to the same linked list of data items. As a result, changes to `valueList` also change `testList`, clearly violating the constraints of call by value. In addition, when the function terminates, the List class destructor is called to delete the copy (`valueList`). As it deletes `valueList`'s linked list of data items, the destructor also is deleting `testList`'s data.

Fortunately, C++ provides us with a method for addressing this problem. We can specify exactly how a copy is to be created by including a **copy constructor** in our List class. The compiler then uses our copy constructor in place of its default (bitwise) copy constructor.

Classes that have problems because of the default copying behavior also encounter similar problems when assigning one object to another. This is solved in C++ by overloading the assignment operator ('='). A number of other operators, for example, the comparison operator ('=='), also do not function as expected because they do a bitwise comparison of the pointers instead of comparing the data that the pointers reference.

These problems arise because of a failure to distinguish between identical data and equivalent data. To help put this into perspective, imagine that you are at a pizza restaurant. The waiter comes to your table and asks if you are ready to order. You are in a hurry, so you glance around and notice that the pizza at the next table looks good. You tell the waiter, "I'll have what they're having." Imagine the surprise if the waiter were to walk over to the next table, pick up their pizza, and put it down on your table for you to eat. You had probably meant that you wanted to have an *equivalent* pizza, not the very same identical pizza.

Although this is not a perfect analogy, when C++ needs to make a copy of a data structure, it does what the waiter did and tries to give you an exact copy. By default, the C++ compiler works with a **shallow** version of the data structure in which the values of the pointers are treated as the real data to be copied or compared—a copy is identical. Instead, we need to work with a **deep** version of the data structure—the values of the pointers must be dereferenced to find the actual data structure items that need to be copied or compared. Initialized objects should end up containing equivalent data. We can ensure correct program behavior by providing copy constructors and overloading the necessary operators. Note that if you do not provide a copy constructor and overload the assignment operator, your program is likely to fail with strange and hard-to-diagnose errors involving memory references. The rule of thumb for deciding whether or not you need to provide a copy constructor and overloaded assignment operator is as follows:

If the class contains pointers and performs dynamic memory allocation, you should—at a minimum—implement the copy constructor and overload the assignment operator.

It is possible to learn all the situations under which the problems can arise—such as passing a list object as a value parameter—and try to avoid those situations, but it is very easy to make mistakes. Do not take shortcuts. Failure to implement the copy constructor and overloaded assignment operator will come back to haunt you.

The prototype for the copy constructor for an arbitrary class, C, is as follows:

```
C ( const C &value );
```

The object `value` is what the constructor must use to initialize the local data. Although the data in `value` is probably private, this is not a problem for the constructor code because objects of a given class are permitted to access all parts of another object of the same class.

The prototype for the overloaded assignment operator is as follows:

```
void operator = ( const C &value );
```

The function behavior here will be almost identical to that of the copy constructor. The differences stem from the fact that with the copy constructor we are initializing a new—not previously initialized—object, whereas with the overloaded assignment operator we are reinitializing an already initialized object. Care must be taken during reinitialization to avoid causing memory leaks and other problems. Note that there is another permissible version of the prototype for the overloaded assignment operator that does not have a `void` return type. It will be discussed in Postlab Exercise 1.

Copy constructors are activated in the following three contexts:

- Objects passed by value to a function. The compiler activates the copy constructor to initialize the function's local temporary copy of the object.
- Object definition with copy initialization. For example, a new list is defined and is to be immediately initialized to be equivalent to another list.

```
List<char> list2 ( list1 );
```

There are object definition situations that activate a copy constructor even though it doesn't look like object definition with copy initialization. For instance, the statement

```
List<char> list2 = list1;
```

activates the copy constructor, not the assignment operation. For reasons partially covered in In-lab Exercise 3, the assignment operation is not used when a variable is initialized in its definition.

- Objects returned by value from a function. Whenever a class object is returned by value from a function, the compiler calls the copy constructor to initialize the receiving storage.

```
list2 = buildList( );
```

where the prototype of `buildList()` is something like the following:

```
List<char> buildList();
```

Note: The preceding section is based in part on material from *Object-Oriented Programming in C++*, Johnsonbaugh and Kalin, 1995, Prentice Hall. This is an extremely useful book for developing an in-depth knowledge of C++.

Enhanced List ADT

Data Items

The data items in a list are of generic type DT.

Structure

The Enhanced List ADT is based on the standard singly linked list presented in Lab 7.

Operations

```
List ( const List<DT> &valueList ) throw ( bad_alloc )
```

Requirements:
None

Results:
Copy constructor. Creates a copy of `valueList`. This constructor automatically is invoked whenever a list is passed to a function using call by value, a function returns a list, or a list is initialized using another list.

```
void operator = ( const List<DT> &rightList ) throw ( bad_alloc )
```

Requirements:
None

Results:
Assigns (copies) the contents of `rightList` to a list.

Laboratory 8: Cover Sheet

Name _____ Date _____

Section _____

Place a check mark in the *Assigned* column next to the exercises your instructor has assigned to you. Attach this cover sheet to the front of the packet of materials you submit following the laboratory.

Activities	Assigned: Check or list exercise numbers	Completed
Prelab Exercise		
Bridge Exercise		
In-lab Exercise 1		
In-lab Exercise 2		
In-lab Exercise 3		
Postlab Exercise 1		
Postlab Exercise 2		
Total		

Laboratory 8: Prelab Exercise

Name _____   Date _____

Section _____

In this laboratory you will create a copy constructor and overload the assignment operator for the singly linked list implementation of the list ADT.

Step 1: Test the (default) copy constructor and assignment operator for your singly linked implementation of the List ADT (Lab 7) using a copy of your *listlnk.cpp* that you should save in the file *listlnk2.cpp*. Also use the provided Lab 8 *listlnk2.h* and the test program given in the file *test8.cpp*. What happens? Why?

Step 2: Implement the List ADT copy constructor and assignment operator using the singly linked implementation of the List ADT (Lab 7) that you have stored in *listlnk2.cpp*. The following declaration for the singly linked list class is given in the file *listlnk2.h*.

```
template < class DT >            // Forward declaration of the List class
class List;

template < class DT >
class ListNode                   // Facilitator class for the List class
{
  private:

    // Constructor
    ListNode ( const DT &nodeData, ListNode *nextPtr );

    // Data members
    DT dataItem;       // List data item
    ListNode *next;    // Pointer to the next list node

  friend class List<DT>;
};

//-------------------------------------------------------------------

template < class DT >
class List
{
  public:

    // Constructors
    List ( int ignored = 0 );
    List ( const List<DT> &srcList )          // Copy constructor
          throw ( bad_alloc );
```

```
    // Destructor
    ~List ();

    void operator= ( const List<DT> &srcList )
        throw ( bad_alloc );

    // List manipulation operations
    void insert ( const DT &newData )          // Insert after cursor
        throw ( bad_alloc );
    void remove ()                             // Remove data item
        throw ( logic_error );
    void replace ( const DT &newData )         // Replace data item
        throw ( logic_error );
    void clear ();                             // Clear list

    // List status operations
    bool isEmpty () const;                     // List is empty
    bool isFull () const;                      // List is full

    // List iteration operations
    void gotoBeginning ()                      // Go to beginning
        throw ( logic_error );
    void gotoEnd ()                            // Go to end
        throw ( logic_error );
    bool gotoNext ()
        throw ( logic_error )                  // Go to next data item
    bool gotoPrior ()
        throw ( logic_error );                 // Go to prior item
    DT getCursor () const                      // Return item
        throw ( logic_error );

    // Output the list structure — used in testing/debugging
    void showStructure () const;

  private:

    // Data members
    ListNode<DT> *head,     // Pointer to the beginning of the list
                 *cursor;   // Cursor pointer
};
```

Laboratory 8: Bridge Exercise

Name _____ Date _____

Section _____

Check with your instructor whether you are to complete this exercise prior to your lab period or during lab.

The test program in the file *test8.cpp* allows you to interactively test your implementation of the Enhanced List ADT using the following commands.

Command	Action
+x	Insert data item x after the cursor.
N	Go to the next data item.
P	Go to the prior data item.
C	Test the copy constructor.
=	Test the assignment operator.
!	Double check the assignment operator.
Q	Quit the test program.

Step 1: Prepare a test plan for your implementation of the List ADT. Be sure to test that your copy constructor and assignment operator work with empty lists. A test plan form follows.

Step 2: Implement your new functions in the file *listlnk2.cpp*.

Step 3: Execute the test plan. If you discover mistakes in your implementation of the copy constructor and assignment operator, correct them and execute the test plan again.

Test Plan for the New Operations in the Enhanced List ADT

Test Case	Commands	Expected Result	Checked

Laboratory 8: In-lab Exercise 1

Name _____ Date _____

Section _____

You are now familiar with the copy constructor and have the knowledge to decide when there is a need to implement your own copy constructor. C++ also permits the definition of other constructors that, although nonessential, can be extremely useful.

A **convert constructor** allows you to initialize an object by passing an object of a different type. You have probably already used this with the C++ string class as given in the following example,

```
string lastName( "Smith" );
```

the C-string "Smith"—of a different type than `string`—is used to initialize the string object.

Convert constructors can be used with a wide range of initialization types. To give you experience implementing a convert constructor, we will ask you to create one for the singly linked implementation of the List ADT that will accept a Logbook as the initializer. For the purposes of this exercise, assume the list contains integers.

```
List ( const Logbook &log )
```

Requirements:
Log is a valid logbook.

Results:
Constructor. Creates a list representation of the logbook containing appropriate entries for the logbook month, year, number of days in the month, and each of the days in the month.

Step 1: Copy *logbook.h* and *logbook.cpp* to your Lab 8 directory. Modify the *listlnk2.h* file to include *logbook.h* and insert the convert constructor prototype underneath the other constructor declarations in the List class declaration.

Step 2: Implement the convert constructor described above and add it to the file *listlnk2.cpp*.

Step 3: Copy the file *test-convert.cs* to *test-convert.cpp*. The first half of the program is provided from the Lab 1 prelab and allows the user to enter data into a logbook. The second half of the program starts with the following lines:

```
// Create a list to represent the logbook and display
// the log using the singly-linked list.
List<int> logList( testLog );

cout << endl
     << "Now printing same logbook from linked list" << endl;
```

```
// Insert your code below. It should include the month, year,
// number of days in the month, and a printout of the logbook
// data from logList identical to the logbook listings above.
// All the necessary data from testLog should now be in
// logList—do NOT use testLog from here on.
```

LogList should now contain all the information that testLog contains. Use only logList to implement the missing part of the program. Your added code should produce the following output.

```
Now printing same logbook from linked list

Logbook created for Month : 8, Year  : 2002
# days in month : 31

1  1      2  2      3  3      4  4      5  0
6  0      7  0      8  0      9  0      10 0
11 0      12 0      13 0      14 0      15 0
16 0      17 0      18 0      19 0      20 0
21 0      22 0      23 0      24 0      25 0
26 0      27 0      28 0      29 0      30 30
31 31
```

Step 4: Complete the test plan for the convert constructor and the code you added to print out the logbook data.

Step 5: Execute the test plan. If you discover mistakes in your implementation of the convert constructor or your logbook data display, correct them and execute the test plan again.

Test Plan for the Convert Constructor and Test Program

Test Case	Logbook Month	# Days in Month	Checked
Simple month	1 2003	31	
Month in the past	7 1969		
Month in the future	12 2011		
February (nonleap year)	2 2003		
February (leap year)	2 2004		

Laboratory 8: In-lab Exercise 2

Name _____ Date _____

Section _____

We have examined how the behavior of the default C++ copy constructor and assignment operator can cause run-time errors and cause the program to halt in mid-execution. Less catastrophic—but still unacceptable—behavior is exhibited by a number of the other default C++ operators whenever the deep version of the data structure must be used instead of the shallow version. For instance, the comparison operator ('==') gives invalid results when comparing two equivalent but distinct singly linked lists because it compares the values of the head and cursor pointers instead of comparing the data items in the lists.

```
bool operator == ( const List &rightList )
```

Requirements:
None

Results:
Compares the deep structure values of a list to that of rightList. If they are the same—that is, equivalent values—then returns true. Otherwise, returns false.

Step 1: Implement this operation and add it to the file *listlnk2.cpp*. A prototype for this operation is included in the declaration of the List class in the file *listlnk2.h*.

Step 2: Activate the '?' (equal?) command in the test program in the file *test8.cpp* by removing the comment delimiter (and the character '?') from the lines that begin with '//?'.

Step 3: Prepare a test plan that covers various lists, including empty lists and lists containing a single data item. Note that you can set the value of the second list in the test program by using the '=' command. A test plan form follows.

Step 4: Execute your test plan. If you discover mistakes in your implementation of the reverse operation, correct them and execute your test plan again.

Test Plan for Test ? (Equality Comparison Operation)

Test Case	Commands	Expected Result	Checked

Laboratory 8: In-lab Exercise 3

Name _____ Date _____

Section _____

In complex programs with pointers, it is possible to have multiple references to the same object. Although probably not intended, it is possible to accidentally write a C++ statement assigning an object to itself. A statement such as

```
list1 = list1;
```

is not likely to be written by a programmer and would most likely be removed by an optimizing compiler as a useless statement. However, it might be possible to have a C++ statement like

```
List<int> *listPtr;
listPtr = &list1;
// Intermediate statements
. . .
*listPtr = list1;
```

that *would* sneak past the optimizer. This code is assigning the list to itself.

The main problem here is not that the C++ compiler might fail to remove an unneeded statement, but something much more serious.

Step 1: Activate the 's' (test self-assignment) command in the test program in the file *test8.cpp* by removing the comment delimiter (and the character 's') from the lines beginning with "//s".

Step 2: Compile *test8.cpp* and run the executable. Place some data into the list and then choose the 's' command. What happens? Why did it happen?

The copy constructor is run to initialize a new object and consequently there is no need to clear out previous data. The problem that occurs with the assignment operation is that the list is already initialized and may contain data. Before the list can be reinitialized, any existing data must be removed properly by returning the list nodes to the memory manager. The next step is to have the list initialize itself to itself, but it just finished deallocating all of its nodes, leaving nothing to copy.

The solution is to verify that the object is not copying from itself. This can be easily achieved by using the pointer named this that the C++ compiler places in each object and initializes to the address of the object. Because each object has a unique memory address, an object can verify whether or not it is the same as another object by comparing the contents of this to the address of the other object.

Step 3: Complete the following test plan by adding test cases that check whether your implementation of the assignment operation correctly handles the assignment to self problem.

Step 4: Modify your `operator=()` function in *listlnk2.cpp* so that no harm is done if the list is passed itself as the initialization model.

Step 5: Execute your test plan. If you discover mistakes in your implementation of these operations, correct them and execute your test plan again.

Test Plan for the Corrected Assignment Operation

Test Case	Commands	Expected Result	Checked

Laboratory 8: Postlab Exercise 1

Name _____ Date _____

Section _____

There are two possible prototypes for the overloaded assignment operator. The one used in the prelab is

```
void operator = ( const List<DT> &rightList )
```

Given three list objects—list1, list2, and list3—you set list2 and list3 to the same value as list1 as follows:

```
list2 = list1;
list3 = list1;
```

The other prototype for the assignment operator changes the return type from void to List<DT>& as follows:

```
List<DT>& operator = ( const List<DT> &rightList )
```

The List<DT>& is a reference to the list that can be used in further expressions such as multiple assignments on the same line. For instance, this permits

```
list3 = list2 = list1;
```

and

```
if (( list2 = list1 ) == list3 )
```

The code for the two versions of the function are identical except for the last line on the second version—the one with return type List<DT>&. As mentioned in In-lab 3, every object has a compiler-generated pointer named this that contains the object's address. To return a reference to the object, the second function adds the line

```
return *this;
```

Which version of the assignment operator function is preferable? Explain your reasoning.

Laboratory 8: Postlab Exercise 2

Name _____ Date _____

Section _____

Consider all the ADTs covered so far in this lab book—Logbook (1), Point List (2), Array implementation of the List (3), Ordered List (4), Stack (5), Queue (6), and Singly linked Implementation of the List (7). Which of them need to have a copy constructor and an overloaded assignment operator? Explain your reasoning.

Doubly Linked List Implementation of the List ADT

In this laboratory you will:

■ Implement the List ADT using a doubly linked list

■ Create an anagram puzzle program

■ Reverse a linked list

■ Analyze the efficiency of your doubly linked list implementation of the List ADT

Objectives

Overview

The singly linked list implementation of the List ADT that you created in Laboratory 7 is quite efficient when it comes to insertion and movement from one node to the next. It is not nearly so efficient, however, when it comes to deletion and movement backward through the list. In this laboratory, you create an implementation of the List ADT using a circular, doubly linked list. This implementation performs most of the List ADT operations in constant time.

List ADT

Data Items

The data items in a list are of generic type DT.

Structure

The data items form a linear structure in which list data items follow one after the other, from the beginning of the list to its end. The ordering of the data items is determined by when and where each data item is inserted into the list and is *not* a function of the data contained in the list data items. At any point in time, one data item in any nonempty list is marked using the list's cursor. You travel through the list using operations that change the position of the cursor.

Operations

```
List ( int ignored = 0 )
```

Requirements:
None

Results:
Constructor. Creates an empty list. The argument is provided for call compatibility with the array implementation and is ignored.

```
~List ()
```

Requirements:
None

Results:
Destructor. Deallocates (frees) the memory used to store a list.

```
void insert ( const DT &newDataItem ) throw ( bad_alloc )
```

Requirements:
List is not full.

Results:
Inserts `newDataItem` into a list. If the list is not empty, then inserts `newDataItem` after the cursor. Otherwise, inserts `newDataItem` as the first (and only) data item in the list. In either case, moves the cursor to `newDataItem`.

```
void remove () throw ( logic_error )
```

Requirements:
List is not empty.

Results:
Removes the data item marked by the cursor from a list. If the resulting list is not empty, then moves the cursor to the data item that followed the deleted data item. If the deleted data item was at the end of the list, then moves the cursor to the beginning of the list.

```
void replace ( const DT &newDataItem ) throw ( logic_error )
```

Requirements:
List is not empty.

Results:
Replaces the `dataItem` marked by the cursor with `newDataItem`. The cursor remains at `newDataItem`.

```
void clear ()
```

Requirements:
None

Results:
Removes all the data items in a list.

```
bool isEmpty () const
```

Requirements:
None

Results:
Returns `true` if a list is empty. Otherwise, returns `false`.

```
bool isFull () const
```

Requirements:
None

Results:
Returns `true` if a list is full. Otherwise, returns `false`.

```
void gotoBeginning () throw ( logic_error )
```

Requirements:
List is not empty.

Results:
Moves the cursor to the beginning of the list.

```
void gotoEnd () throw ( logic_error )
```

Requirements:
List is not empty.

Results:
Moves the cursor to the end of the list.

```
bool gotoNext () throw ( logic_error )
```

Requirements:
List is not empty.

Results:
If the cursor is not at the end of a list, then moves the cursor to the next data item in the list and returns `true`. Otherwise, returns `false`.

```
bool gotoPrior () throw ( logic_error )
```

Requirements:
List is not empty.

Results:
If the cursor is not at the beginning of a list, then moves the cursor to the preceding data item in the list and returns `true`. Otherwise, returns `false`.

```
DT getCursor () const throw ( logic_error )
```

Requirements:
List is not empty.

Results:
Returns a copy of the data item marked by the cursor.

```
void showStructure () const
```

Requirements:
None

Results:
Outputs the data items in a list. If the list is empty, outputs "Empty list". Note that this operation is intended for testing/debugging purposes only. It supports only list data items that are one of C++'s predefined data types (`int`, `char`, and so forth).

Laboratory 9: Cover Sheet

Name _____   Date _____

Section _____

Place a check mark in the *Assigned* column next to the exercises your instructor has assigned to you. Attach this cover sheet to the front of the packet of materials you submit following the laboratory.

Activities	Assigned: Check or list exercise numbers	Completed
Prelab Exercise		
Bridge Exercise		
In-lab Exercise 1		
In-lab Exercise 2		
In-lab Exercise 3		
Postlab Exercise 1		
Postlab Exercise 2		
Total		

Laboratory 9: Prelab Exercise

Name _____ Date _____

Section _____

Each node in a doubly linked list contains a pair of pointers. One pointer points to the node that precedes the node (prior) and the other points to the node that follows the node (next). The resulting ListNode class is similar to the one you used in Laboratory 7.

```cpp
template < class DT >
class ListNode               // Facilitator class for the List class
{
  private:

    // Constructor
    ListNode ( const DT &data,
               ListNode *priorPtr, ListNode *nextPtr );

    // Data members
    DT dataItem;         // List data item
    ListNode *prior,     // Pointer to the previous data item
             *next;      // Pointer to the next data item

  friend class List<DT>;
};
```

In a circular, doubly linked list, the nodes at the beginning and end of the list are linked together. The next pointer of the node at the end of the list points to the node at the beginning, and the prior pointer of the node at the beginning points to the node at the end.

Step 1: Implement the operations in the List ADT using a circular, doubly linked list. Base your implementation on the class declarations in the file *listdbl.h*. An implementation of the showStructure operation is given in the file *show9.cpp*.

Step 2: Save your implementation of the List ADT in the file *listdbl.cpp*. Be sure to document your code.

Laboratory 9: Bridge Exercise

Name _____ Date _____

Section _____

Check with your instructor whether you are to complete this exercise prior to your lab period or during lab.

The test program in the file *test9.cpp* allows you to interactively test your implementation of the List ADT using the following commands.

Command	Action
+x	Insert data item x after the cursor.
-	Remove the data item marked by the cursor.
=x	Replace the data item marked by the cursor with data item x.
@	Display the data item marked by the cursor.
N	Go to the next data item.
P	Go to the prior data item.
<	Go to the beginning of the list.
>	Go to the end of the list.
E	Report whether the list is empty.
F	Report whether the list is full.
C	Clear the list.
Q	Quit the test program.

Step 1: Prepare a test plan for your implementation of the List ADT. Your test plan should cover the application of each operation to data items at the beginning, middle, and end of lists (where appropriate). A test plan form follows.

Step 2: Execute your test plan. If you discover mistakes in your implementation of the List ADT, correct them and execute your test plan again.

Test Plan for the Operations in the List ADT

Test Case	Commands	Expected Result	Checked

Laboratory 9: In-lab Exercise 1

Name _____   Date _____

Section _____

Lists can be used as data members in other classes. In this exercise, you will create an implementation of the Anagram Puzzle ADT described below using lists of characters to store both the solution to the puzzle and the current puzzle configuration.

Anagram Puzzle ADT

Data Items

Alphabetic characters.

Structure

The characters are arranged linearly. If rearranged properly they spell a specified English word.

Operations

```
AnagramPuzzle ( char answ[], char init[] )
```

Requirements:
Strings `answ` and `init` are nonempty and contain the same letters (but in a different order).

Results:
Constructor. Creates an anagram puzzle. String `answ` is the solution to the puzzle and string `init` is the initial scrambled letter sequence.

```
void shiftLeft ()
```

Requirements:
None

Results:
Shifts the letters in a puzzle left one position. The leftmost letter is moved to the right end of the puzzle.

```
void swapEnds ()
```

Requirements:
None

Results:
Swaps the letters at the left and right ends of a puzzle.

```
void display ()
```

Requirements:
None

Results:
Displays an anagram puzzle.

```
bool solved ()
```

Requirements:
None

Results:
Returns `true` if a puzzle is solved. Otherwise returns `false`.

The following code fragment declares a puzzle in which the word "yes" is scrambled as "yse". It then shows how the puzzle is unscrambled to form "yes".

```
AnagramPuzzle enigma("yes","yse");    // Word is "yes", start w/ "yse"
enigma.shiftLeft();                   // Changes puzzle to "sey"
enigma.swapEnds();                    // Changes puzzle to "yes"
```

Rather than having the solution to the puzzle encoded in the program, your puzzle program allows the user to solve the puzzle by entering commands from the keyboard.

Step 1: Complete the anagram puzzle program shell given in the file *puzzle.cs* by creating an implementation of the Anagram Puzzle ADT. Base your implementation on the following declaration.

```
class AnagramPuzzle
{
  public:

    AnagramPuzzle( char answ[], char init[] );   // Construct puzzle
    void shiftLeft();                            // Shift letters left
    void swapEnds();                             // Swap end letters
    void display();                              // Display puzzle
    bool isSolved();                             // Puzzle solved

  private:

    // Data members
    List<char> solution,    // Solution to puzzle
               puzzle;      // Current puzzle configuration
};
```

Use your circular, doubly linked list implementation of the List ADT to represent the lists of characters storing the puzzle's solution and its current configuration.

Step 2: Test your anagram puzzle program using the puzzles given in the following test plan.

Test Plan for the Anagram Puzzle Program

Test Case	Checked
Puzzle word "yes", scrambled as "yse"	
Puzzle word "right", scrambled as "irtgh"	

Laboratory 9: In-lab Exercise 2

Name _____   Date _____

Section _____

A list can be reversed in two ways: either you can relink the nodes in the list into a new (reversed) order, or you can leave the node structure intact and exchange data items between pairs of nodes. Use one of these strategies to implement the following List ADT operation.

```
void reverse ()
```

Requirements:
None

Results:
Reverses the order of the data items in a list. The cursor does not move.

Step 1: Implement this operation and add it to the file *listdbl.cpp*. A prototype for this operation is included in the declaration of the List class in the file *listdbl.h*.

Step 2: Activate the 'R' (reverse) command in the test program in the file *test9.cpp* by removing the comment delimiter (and the character 'R') from the lines that begin with "//R".

Step 3: Prepare a test plan for the reverse operation that covers lists of various lengths, including lists containing a single data item. A test plan form follows.

Step 4: Execute your test plan. If you discover mistakes in your implementation of the reverse operation, correct them and execute your test plan again.

Test Plan for the Reverse Operation

Test Case	Commands	Expected Result	Checked

Laboratory 9: In-lab Exercise 3

Name _____ Date _____

Section _____

In many list applications you need to know the number of data items in a list and the relative position of the cursor. Rather than computing these attributes each time they are requested, you can store this information in a pair of data members that you update whenever you insert data items, remove data items, or move the cursor.

Step 1: Add the following data members (both are of type `int`) to the List class declaration in the file *listdbl.h* and save the result in the file *listdbl2.h*.

   `size:` The number of data items in a list.

   `pos:` The numeric position of the cursor, where the list data items are numbered from beginning to end, starting with 0.

Step 2: Modify the routines in your circular, doubly linked list implementation of the List ADT so that they update these data members whenever necessary. Save your modified implementation in the file *listdbl2.cpp*.

Step 3: If you are to reference the `size` and `pos` data members within applications programs, you must have List ADT operations that return these values. Add prototypes for the following operations to the List class declaration in the file *listdbl2.h*.

```
int getLength () const
```

Requirements:
None

Results:
Returns the number of data items in a list.

```
int getPosition () const throw ( logic_error )
```

Requirements:
List is not empty.

Results:
Returns the position of the cursor, where the list data items are numbered from beginning to end, starting with 0.

Step 4: Implement these operations and add them to the file *listdbl2.cpp*.

Step 5: Modify the test program in the file *test9.cpp* so that the routines that incorporate your changes (in *listdbl2.cpp*) are included in place of those you created in the Prelab.

Step 6: Activate the '#' (length and position) command by removing the comment delimiter (and the character '#') from the lines that begin with "//#".

Step 7: Prepare a test plan for these operations that checks the length of various lists (including the empty list) and the numeric position of data items at the beginning, middle, and end of lists. A test plan form follows.

Step 8: Execute your test plan. If you discover mistakes in your implementation of these operations, correct them and execute your test plan again.

Test Plan for the Length and Position Operations

Test Case	Commands	Expected Result	Checked

Laboratory 9: Postlab Exercise 1

Name _____ Date _____

Section _____

Part A

Given a list containing N data items, develop worst-case, order-of-magnitude estimates of the execution time of the following List ADT operations, assuming they are implemented using a circular, doubly linked list. Briefly explain your reasoning behind each estimate.

insert   O(   )

Explanation:

remove   O(   )

Explanation:

gotoPrior   O(   )

Explanation:

gotoEnd   O(   )

Explanation:

Part B

Would these estimates be the same for an implementation of the List ADT based on a noncircular, doubly linked list? Explain why or why not.

Laboratory 9: Postlab Exercise 2

Name _____ Date _____

Section _____

Part A

Given the following arbitrarily selected—but plausible—memory requirements and a list containing N integers, compare the amount of memory used by your singly linked list representation of the list (Laboratory 7) with the amount of memory used by your circular, doubly linked list representation.

Character   1 byte

Integer   2 bytes

Address (pointer)   4 bytes

Part B

Suppose the list contains N objects of class Slide (Laboratory 7, In-lab Exercise 1). Compare the amount of memory used by your singly linked list representation of the list with the amount of memory used by your circular, doubly linked representation.

Recursion with Linked Lists

In this laboratory you will:

■ Examine how recursion can be used to traverse a linked list in either direction

■ Use recursion to insert, delete, and move data items in a linked list

■ Convert recursive routines to iterative form

■ Analyze why a stack is sometimes needed when converting from recursive to iterative form

Overview

Recursive functions, or functions that call themselves, provide an elegant way of describing and implementing the solutions to a wide range of problems, including problems in mathematics, computer graphics, compiler design, and artificial intelligence. Let's begin by examining how you develop a recursive function definition, using the factorial function as an example.

You can express the factorial of a positive integer n using the following iterative formula:

$$n! = n \cdot (n - 1) \cdot (n - 2) \cdot \ldots \cdot 1$$

Applying this formula to 4! yields the product $4 \times 3 \times 2 \times 1$. If you regroup the terms in this product as $4 \times (3 \times 2 \times 1)$ and note that $3! = 3 \times 2 \times 1$, then you find that 4! can be written as $4 \times (3!)$. You can generalize this reasoning to form the following recursive definition of factorial:

$$n! = n \cdot (n - 1)!$$

where 0! is defined to be 1. Applying this definition to the evaluation of 4! yields the following sequence of computations.

$$4! = 4 \cdot (3!)$$
$$= 4 \cdot (3 \cdot (2!))$$
$$= 4 \cdot (3 \cdot (2 \cdot (1!)))$$
$$= 4 \cdot (3 \cdot (2 \cdot (1 \cdot (0!))))$$
$$= 4 \cdot (3 \cdot (2 \cdot (1 \cdot (1))))$$

The first four steps in this computation are recursive, with $n!$ being evaluated in terms of $(n - 1)!$. The final step $(0! = 1)$ is not recursive, however. The following notation clearly distinguishes between the **recursive step** and the nonrecursive step (or **base case**) in the definition of $n!$.

$$n! = \begin{cases} 1 & \text{if } n = 0 \text{ (base case)} \\ n \bullet (n - 1)! & \text{if } n > 0 \text{ (recursive step)} \end{cases}$$

The following `factorial()` function uses recursion to compute the factorial of a number.

```
long factorial ( int n )
// Computes n! using recursion.
{
    long result;   // Result returned

    if ( n == 0 )
        result = 1;                    // Base case
    else
        result = n * factorial(n-1);   // Recursive step
    return result;
}
```

Let's look at the call `factorial(4)`. Because 4 is not equal to 0 (the condition for the base case), the `factorial()` function issues the recursive call `factorial(3)`. The recursive calls continue until the base case is reached—that is, until *n* equals 0.

```
factorial(4)
      ↓ RECURSIVE STEP
    4*factorial(3)
              ↓ RECURSIVE STEP
          3*factorial(2)
                  ↓ RECURSIVE STEP
              2*factorial(1)
                      ↓ RECURSIVE STEP
                  1*factorial(0)
                          ↓ BASE CASE
                          1
```

The calls to `factorial()` are evaluated in the reverse of the order they are made. The evaluation process continues until the value 24 is returned by the call `factorial(4)`.

```
factorial(4)
        ↑ RESULT 24
    4*factorial(3)
            ↑ RESULT 6
        3*factorial(2)
                ↑ RESULT 2
            2*factorial(1)
                    ↑ RESULT 1
                1*factorial(0)
                        ↑ RESULT 1
                        1
```

Recursion can be used for more than numerical calculations, however. The following pair of functions traverse a linked list, outputting the data items encountered along the way.

```
template < class DT >
void List<DT>:: write () const

// Outputs the data items in a list from beginning to end. Assumes that
// objects of type DT can be output to the cout stream.

{
    cout << "List : ";
    writeSub(head);
    cout << endl;
}

// - - - - - - - - - - - - - - - - - - - - - - - - - - - - - - - - - - - - -

template < class DT >
void List<DT>:: writeSub ( ListNode<DT> *p ) const

// Recursive partner of the write() function. Processes the sublist
// that begins with the node pointed to by p.
```

```
{
    if ( p != 0 )
    {
        cout << p->dataItem;        // Output data item
        writeSub(p->next);          // Continue with next node
    }
}
```

The role of the `write()` function is to initiate the recursive process, which is then carried forward by its recursive partner the `writeSub()` function. Calling `write()` with the linked list of characters

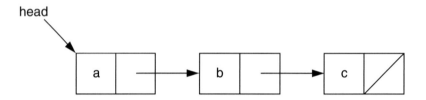

yields the following sequence of calls and outputs "abc".

```
writeSub(head)
        ↓ RECURSIVE STEP
    Output 'a'    writeSub(p->next)
                        ↓RECURSIVE STEP
                Output 'b'    writeSub(p->next)
                                    ↓RECURSIVE STEP
                            Output 'c'    writeSub(p->next)
                                                ↓ BASE CASE
                                            No output
```

Recursion also can be used to add nodes to a linked list. The following pair of functions insert a data item at the end of a list.

```
template < class DT >
void List<DT>:: insertEnd ( const DT &newDataItem )

// Inserts newDataItem at the end of a list. Moves the cursor to
// newDataItem.

{
    insertEndSub(head,newDataItem);
}

// - - - - - - - - - - - - - - - - - - - - - - - - - - - - - - - - -

template < class DT >
void List<DT>:: insertEndSub ( ListNode<DT> *&p,
                               const DT &newDataItem )

// Recursive partner of the insertEnd() function. Processes the
// sublist that begins with the node pointed to by p.

{
    if ( p != 0 )
        insertEndSub(p->next,newDataItem);      // Continue searching for
```

```
    else                                     // end of list
    {
        p = new ListNode<DT>(newDataItem,0);  // Insert new node
        cursor = p;                           // Move cursor
    }
}
```

The `insertEnd()` function initiates the insertion process, with the bulk of the work being done by its recursive partner, the `insertEndSub()` function. Calling `insertEnd()` to insert the character '!' at the end of the following list of characters:

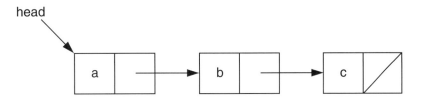

yields the following sequence of calls.

```
insertEndSub(head)
        ↓RECURSIVE STEP
insertEndSub(p->next)
        ↓RECURSIVE STEP
insertEndSub(p->next)
        ↓RECURSIVE STEP
insertEndSub(p->next)
        ↓BASE CASE
Create a new node containing '!'
```

On the last call, `p` is null and the statement

```
p = new ListNode<LE>(newDataItem,0);    // Insert new node
```

is executed to create a new node containing the character '!'. The address of this node is then assigned to `p`. Because `p` is passed using call by reference, this assignment changes the next pointer of the last node in the list ('c') to point to the new node, thereby producing the following list:

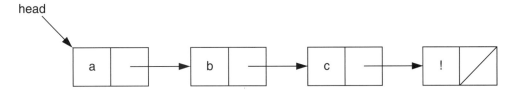

Calling `insertEnd()` to insert the character '!' into an empty list results in a single call to the `insertEndSub()` function.

```
insertEndSub(head)
        ↓RECURSIVE STEP
Create a new node containing '!'
```

In this case, assigning the address of the newly created node to p changes the list's head pointer to point to this node.

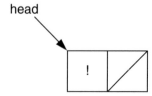

Note that the insertEnd() function automatically links the node it creates into either an existing list or an empty list without the use of special tests to determine whether the insertion changes a node's next pointer or the list's head pointer. The key is that parameter p is passed using call by reference.

Laboratory 10: Cover Sheet

Name _____   Date _____

Section _____

Place a check mark in the *Assigned* column next to the exercises your instructor has assigned to you. Attach this cover sheet to the front of the packet of materials you submit following the laboratory.

Activities	Assigned: Check or list exercise numbers	Completed
Prelab Exercise		
Bridge Exercise		
In-lab Exercise 1		
In-lab Exercise 2		
In-lab Exercise 3		
Postlab Exercise 1		
Postlab Exercise 2		
Total		

Laboratory 10: Prelab Exercise

Name _____ Date _____

Section _____

We begin by examining a set of recursive functions that perform known tasks. These functions are collected in the file *listrec.cs*. You can execute them using the test program in the file *test10.cpp*.

Part A

Step 1: To complete this laboratory, you need to use some of the functions from your singly linked list implementation of the List ADT. Complete the partial implementation of the List ADT in the file *listrec.cs* by adding the following functions from the linked list implementation you developed in Laboratory 7:

- The constructor for the ListNode class.

- The List class constructor, destructor, insert(), clear(), and showStructure() functions. Add any other functions that these depend on.

Prototypes for these functions are included in the declaration of the List class in the file *listrec.h*. Add prototypes for any other functions as needed.

Step 2: Save the resulting implementation in the file *listrec.cpp*.

Step 3: Activate the calls to the write() and insertEnd() functions in the test program in the file *test10.cpp* by removing the comment delimiter (and the characters 'PA') from the lines beginning with "//PA".

Step 4: Execute the write() and insertEnd() functions using the following list.

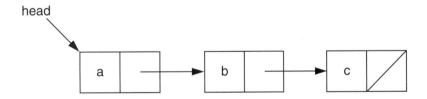

Step 5: What output does write() produce?

Step 6: What list does `insertEnd()` produce?

Step 7: Execute these functions using an empty list.

Step 8: What output does `write()` produce?

Step 9: What list does `insertEnd()` produce?

Part B

One of the most common reasons to use recursion with linked lists is to support traversal of a list from its end back to its beginning. The following pair of functions outputs each list data item twice, once as the list is traversed from beginning to end and again as it is traversed from the end back to the beginning.

```
template < class DT >
void List<DT>:: writeMirror () const

// Outputs the data items in a list from beginning to end and back
// again. Assumes that objects of type DT can be output to the cout
// stream.

{
    cout << "Mirror : ";
    writeMirrorSub(head);
    cout << endl;
}

// - - - - - - - - - - - - - - - - - - - - - - - - - - - - - - - - - -

template < class DT >
void List<DT>:: writeMirrorSub ( ListNode<DT> *p ) const

// Recursive partner of the writeMirror() function. Processes the
// sublist that begins with the node pointed to by p.

{
    if ( p != 0 )
    {
        cout << p->dataItem;        // Output data item (forward)
        writeMirrorSub(p->next);    // Continue with next node
        cout << p->dataItem;        // Output data item (backward)
    }
}
```

Step 1: Activate the call to the `writeMirror()` function in the test program in the file *test10.cpp* by removing the comment delimiter (and the characters 'PB') from the lines beginning with "//PB".

Step 2: Execute the `writeMirror()` function using the following list.

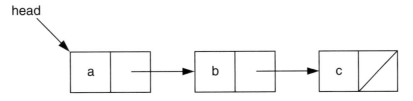

Step 3: What output does `writeMirror()` produce?

Step 4: Describe what each statement in the `writeMirrorSub()` function does during the call in which parameter p points to the node containing 'a'.

Step 5: What is the significance of the call to `writeMirrorSub()` in which parameter p is null?

Step 6: Describe how the calls to `writeMirrorSub()` combine to produce the "mirrored" output. Use a diagram to illustrate your answer.

Part C

The following pair of functions reverse a list by changing each node's `next` pointer. Note that the pointers are changed on the way back through the list.

```
template < class DT >
void List<DT>:: reverse ()

// Reverses the order of the data items in a list.

{
    reverseSub(0,head);
}

// - - - - - - - - - - - - - - - - - - - - - - - - - - - - - - - - - - -

template < class DT >
void List<DT>:: reverseSub ( ListNode<DT> *p, ListNode<DT> *nextP )

// Recursive partner of the reverse() function. Processes the sublist
// that begins with the node pointed to by nextP.

{
    if ( nextP != 0 )
    {
        reverseSub(nextP,nextP->next);    // Continue with next node
        nextP->next = p;                  // Reverse link
    }
    else
        head = p;                         // Move head to end of list
}
```

Step 1: Activate the call to the `reverse()` function in the test program by removing the comment delimiter (and the characters 'PC') from the lines beginning with "//PC".

Step 2: Execute the `reverse()` function using the following list.

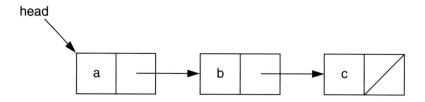

Step 3: What list does `reverse()` produce?

Step 4: Describe what each statement in the reverseSub() function does during the call in which parameter p points to the node containing 'a'. In particular, how are the links to and from this node changed as a result of this call?

Step 5: What is the significance of the call to reverseSub() in which parameter p is null?

Step 6: Describe how the calls to reverseSub() combine to reverse the list. Use a diagram to illustrate your answer.

Part D

In the Overview, you saw how you can use recursion in conjunction with call by reference to insert a node at the end of a list. The following pair of functions use this technique to delete the last node in a list.

```
template < class DT >
void List<DT>:: deleteEnd ()

// Deletes the data item at the end of a list. Moves the cursor to the
// beginning of the list.

{
    deleteEndSub(head);
    cursor = head;
}


// - - - - - - - - - - - - - - - - - - - - - - - - - - - - - - - - - - - - - -


template < class DT >
void List<DT>:: deleteEndSub ( ListNode<DT> *&p )

// Recursive partner of the deleteEnd() function. Processes the
// sublist that begins with the node pointed to by p.

{
    if ( p->next != 0 )
        deleteEndSub(p->next);    // Continue looking for the last node
    else
    {
        delete p;                 // Delete node
        p = 0;                    // Set p (link or head) to null
    }
}
```

Step 1: Activate the call to the `deleteEnd()` function in the test program by removing the comment delimiter (and the characters 'PD') from the lines beginning with "//PD".

Step 2: Execute the `deleteEnd()` function using the following list.

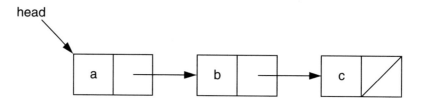

Step 3: What list does `deleteEnd()` produce?

Step 4: What is the significance of the calls to the `deleteEndSub()` function in which `p->next` is not null?

Step 5: Describe what each statement in `deleteEndSub()` does during the call in which `p->next` is null. Use a diagram to illustrate your answer.

Step 6: What list does `deleteEnd()` produce when called with a list containing one data item? Describe how this result is accomplished. Use a diagram to illustrate your answer.

Part E

The following pair of functions determine the length of a list. These functions do not simply count nodes as they move through the list from beginning to end (as an iterative function would). Instead, they use a recursive definition of length in which the length of the list pointed to by pointer p is the length of the list pointed to by p->next (the remaining nodes in the list) plus one (the node pointed to by p).

$$length(p) = \begin{cases} 0 & \text{if } p = 0 \text{ (base case)} \\ length(p\text{->}next) + 1 & \text{if } p \neq 0 \text{ (recursive step)} \end{cases}$$

```
template < class DT >
int List<DT>:: getLength () const

// Returns the number of data items in a list.

{
    return getLengthSub (head);
}

// - - - - - - - - - - - - - - - - - - - - - - - - - - - - - - - -

template < class DT >
int List<DT>:: getLengthSub ( ListNode<DT> *p ) const

// Recursive partner of the getLength() function. Processes the sublist
// that begins with the node pointed to by p.

{
    int result;    // Result returned

    if ( p == 0 )
        result = 0;                                // End of list reached
    else
        result = ( getLengthSub (p->next) + 1 ); // Number of nodes after
                                                 // this one + 1
    return result;
}
```

Step 1: Activate the call to the getLength() function in the test program by removing the comment delimiter (and the characters 'PE') from the lines beginning with "//PE".

Step 2: Execute the getLength() function using the following list.

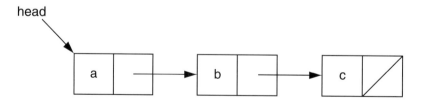

Step 3: What result does `getLength()` produce?

Step 4: What is the significance of the call to the `getLengthSub()` function in which parameter `p` is null?

Step 5: Describe how the calls to `getLengthSub()` combine to return the length of the list. Use a diagram to illustrate your answer.

Step 6: What value does the `getLength()` function return when called with an empty list? Describe how this value is computed. Use a diagram to illustrate your answer.

Laboratory 10: Bridge Exercise

Name _____ Date _____

Section _____

Check with your instructor whether you are to complete this exercise prior to your lab period or during lab.

Part A

The following pair of functions perform some unspecified action.

```
template < class DT >
void List<DT>:: unknown1 () const

// Unknown function 1.

{
    unknown1Sub(head);
    cout << endl;
}

// - - - - - - - - - - - - - - - - - - - - - - - - - - - - - - - -

template < class DT >
void List<DT>:: unknown1Sub ( ListNode<DT> *p ) const

// Recursive partner of the unknown1() function.

{
    if ( p != 0 )
    {
        cout << p->dataItem;
        if ( p->next != 0 )
        {
            unknown1Sub(p->next->next);
            cout << p->next->dataItem;
        }
    }
}
```

Step 1: Activate the call to the `unknown1()` function in the test program in the file *test10.cpp* by removing the comment delimiter (and the characters 'BA') from the lines beginning with "//BA".

Step 2: Execute the unknown1() function using the following list.

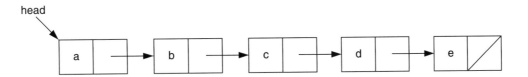

Step 3: What output does unknown1() produce?

Step 4: Describe what each statement in the unknown1Sub() function does during the call in which parameter p points to the node containing 'a'.

Step 5: Describe how the calls to unknown1Sub() combine to output the list. Use a diagram to illustrate your answer.

Part B

The following pair of functions perform yet another unspecified action.

```
template < class DT >
void List<DT>:: unknown2 ()
// Unknown function 2.
{
    unknown2Sub(head);
}

// - - - - - - - - - - - - - - - - - - - - - - - - - - - - - - - - - - - - -
```

```
template < class DT >
void List<DT>:: unknown2Sub ( ListNode<DT> *&p )
// Recursive partner of the unknown2() function.
{
    ListNode<DT> *q;

    if ( p != 0  &&  p->next != 0 )
    {
        q = p;
        p = p->next;
        q->next = p->next;
        p->next = q;
        unknown2Sub(q->next);
    }
}
```

Step 1: Activate the call to the unknown2() function in the test program by removing the comment delimiter (and the characters 'BB') from the lines beginning with "//BB".

Step 2: Execute the unknown2() function using the following list.

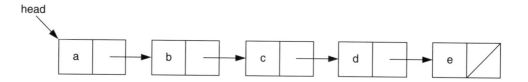

Step 3: What list does unknown2() produce?

Step 4: Describe what each statement in the unknown2Sub() function does during the call in which parameter p points to the node containing 'a'. In particular, what role does the fact that p is passed using call by reference play in this call?

Step 5: Describe how the calls to unknown2Sub() combine to restructure the list. Use a diagram to illustrate your answer.

Laboratory 10: In-lab Exercise 1

Name _____ Date _____

Section _____

Although recursion can be an intuitive means for expressing algorithms, there are times you may wish to replace recursion with iteration. This replacement is most commonly done when analysis of a program's execution reveals that the overhead associated with a particular recursive routine is too costly, either in terms of time or memory usage.

Part A

Replacing recursion in a routine such as the `getLength()` function (Prelab Exercise, Part E) is fairly easy. Rather than using recursive calls to move through the list, you move a pointer of type `ListNode*` from node to node. In the case of the `getLength()` function, this iterative process continues until you reach the end of the list.

The `reverse()` function (Prelab Exercise, Part C) presents a somewhat more challenging problem. The iterative form of this routine moves a set of pointers through the list in a coordinated manner. As these pointers move through the list, they reverse the links between pairs of nodes, thereby reversing the list itself.

Step 1: Create an implementation of the `reverse()` function that uses iteration, in conjunction with a small set of pointers, in place of recursion. Call this function `iterReverse()` and add it to the file *listrec.cpp*. A prototype for this function is included in the declaration of the List class in the file *listrec.h*.

Step 2: Activate the call to the `iterReverse()` function in the test program in the file *test10.cpp* by removing the comment delimiter (and the characters '1A') from the lines beginning with "//1A".

Step 3: Prepare a test plan for the `iterReverse()` function that covers lists of different lengths, including lists containing a single data item. A test plan form follows.

Step 4: Execute your test plan. If you discover mistakes in your `iterReverse()` function, correct them and execute your test plan again.

Test Plan for the `iterReverse` Operation

Test Case	List	Expected Result	Checked

Part B

The `writeMirror()` function (Prelab Exercise, Part B) presents an even greater challenge. The iterative form of this routine uses a stack to store pointers to the nodes in a list. This stack is used in concert with an iterative process of the following form:

```
Stack<ListNode<DT>*> tempStack;    // Stack of pointers
ListNode *p;                       // Iterates through list

Set p to the head of the list.    // Traverse list from
while ( p != 0 ) do                // first to last
{
    tempStack.push(p);
    Process the list node pointed to by p (if necessary).
    Advance p to the next node in the list.
}


while ( !tempStack.isEmpty() ) do // Traverse list from
{                                 // last to first
    p = tempStack.pop();
    Process the list node pointed to by p.
}
```

Step 1: Create an implementation of the `writeMirror()` function that uses iteration, in conjunction with a stack, in place of recursion. Call the resulting function `stackWriteMirror()` and add it to the file *listrec.cpp*. A prototype for this function is included in the declaration of the List class in the file *listrec.h*. Base your `stackWriteMirror()` function on one of your implementations of the Stack ADT from Laboratory 5.

Step 2: Activate the call to the `stackWriteMirror()` function in the test program by removing the comment delimiter (and the characters '1B') from the lines beginning with "//1B".

Step 3: Prepare a test plan for the `stackWriteMirror()` function that covers lists of different lengths, including lists containing a single data item. A test plan form follows.

Step 4: Execute your test plan. If you discover mistakes in your `stackWrite-Mirror()` function, correct them and execute your test plan again.

Test Plan for the `stackWriteMirror` **Operation**

Test Case	List	Expected Result	Checked

Laboratory 10: In-lab Exercise 2

Name _____ Date _____

Section _____

You saw in the Prelab that you can use recursion to insert a data item at the end of a list. You also can use recursion to add data items at the beginning and middle of lists.

```
void aBeforeb ()
```

Requirements:
List contains characters.

Results:
Inserts the character 'a' immediately before each occurrence of the character 'b'. Does not move the cursor.

Step 1: Create an implementation of the `aBeforeb()` function that is based on recursion—*not* iteration—and add your implementation to the file *listrec.cpp*. A prototype for this function is included in the declaration of the List class in the file *listrec.h*.

Step 2: Activate the call to the `aBeforeb()` function in the test program in the file *test10.cpp* by removing the comment delimiter (and the character '2') from the lines beginning with "//2".

Step 3: Prepare a test plan for this function that includes lists containing the character 'b' at the beginning, middle, and end. A test plan form follows.

Step 4: Execute your test plan. If you discover mistakes in your implementation of the `aBeforeb()` function, correct them and execute your test plan again.

Test Plan for the aBeforeb Operation

Test Case	List	Expected Result	Checked

Laboratory 10: In-lab Exercise 3

Name _____   Date _____

Section _____

You saw in the Prelab that you can use recursion to delete the data item at the end of a list. You also can use recursion to express the restructuring required following the deletion of data items at the beginning and middle of lists.

```
void cRemove ()
```

Requirements:
List contains characters.

Results:
Removes all the occurrences of the character 'c' from a list of characters. Moves the cursor to the beginning of the list.

Step 1: Create an implementation of the `cRemove()` function that is based on recursion—*not* iteration—and add it to the file *listrec.cpp*. A prototype for this function is included in the declaration of the List class in the file *listrec.h*.

Step 2: Activate the call to the `cRemove()` function in the test program in the file *test10.cpp* by removing the comment delimiter (and the character '3') from the lines beginning with "//3".

Step 3: Prepare a test plan for this function that includes lists containing the character 'c' at the beginning, middle, and end. A test plan form follows.

Step 4: Execute your test plan. If you discover mistakes in your implementation of the `cRemove()` function, correct them and execute your test plan again.

Test Plan for the `cRemove` Operation

Test Case	List	Expected Result	Checked

Laboratory 10: Postlab Exercise 1

Name _____ Date _____

Section _____

One mistake we sometimes make when we first begin writing recursive routines is to use a `while` loop in place of an if selection structure. Suppose we replace the `if` statement

```
if ( p != 0 )
{
   cout << p->dataItem;      // Output forward
   writeMirrorSub(p->next);  // Continue with next node
   cout << p->dataItem;      // Output backward
}
```

in the `writeMirrorSub()` function (Prelab Exercise, Part B) with the `while` loop

```
while ( p != 0 )
{
   cout << p->dataItem;      // Output forward
   writeMirrorSub(p->next);  // Continue with next node
   cout << p->dataItem;      // Output backward
}
```

What would be the consequence of this change?

Laboratory 10: Postlab Exercise 2

Name _____   Date _____

Section _____

It is often impossible to convert a recursive routine to iterative form without the use of a stack (see In-lab Exercise 1). Explain why a stack is needed in the iterative form of the `writeMirror()` function.

Binary Search Tree ADT

In this laboratory you will:

- Create an implementation of the Binary Search Tree ADT using a linked tree structure

- Examine how an index can be used to retrieve records from a database file and construct an indexing program for an accounts database

- Create operations that compute the height of a tree and output the data items in a tree whose keys are less than a specified key

- Analyze the efficiency of your implementation of the Binary Search Tree ADT

Overview

In this laboratory, you examine how a binary tree can be used to represent the hierarchical search process embodied in the binary search algorithm.

The binary search algorithm allows you to efficiently locate a data item in an array provided that each array data item has a unique identifier, called its **key**, and that the array data items are stored in order based on their keys. Given the following array of keys,

Index	0	1	2	3	4	5	6
Key	16	20	31	43	65	72	86

a binary search for the data item with key 31 begins by comparing 31 with the key in the middle of the array, 43. Because 31 is less than 43, the data item with key 31 must lie in the lower half of the array (entries 0–2). The key in the middle of this subarray is 20. Because 31 is greater than 20, the data item with key 31 must lie in the upper half of this subarray (entry 2). This array entry contains the key 31. Thus, the search terminates with success.

Although the comparisons made during a search for a given key depend on the key, the relative order in which comparisons are made is invariant for a given array of data items. For instance, when searching through the previous array, you always compare the key that you are searching for with 43 before you compare it with either 20 or 72. Similarly, you always compare the key with 72 before you compare it with either 65 or 86. The order of comparisons associated with this array is shown below.

Index	0	1	2	3	4	5	6
Key	16	20	31	43	65	72	86
Order compared	3	2	3	1	3	2	3

The hierarchical nature of the comparisons that are performed by the binary search algorithm is reflected in the following tree.

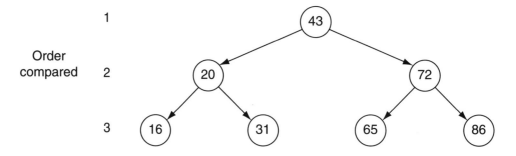

Observe that for each key K in this tree, all of the keys in K's left subtree are less than K and all of the keys in K's right subtree are greater than K. Trees with this property are referred to as **binary search trees**.

When searching for a key in a binary search tree, you begin at the root node and move downward along a branch until either you find the node containing the key or you reach a leaf node without finding the key. Each move along a branch corresponds to an array subdivision in the binary search algorithm. At each node, you move down to the left if the key you are searching for is less than the key stored in the node, or you move down to the right if the key you are searching for is greater than the key stored in the node.

Binary Search Tree ADT

Data Items

The data items in a binary search tree are of generic type DT. Each data item has a key (of generic type KF) that uniquely identifies the data item. Data items usually include additional data. Objects of type KF must support the six basic relational operators. Objects of type DT must provide a functional getKey() that returns a data item's key.

Structure

The data items form a binary tree. For each data item D in the tree, all the data items in D's left subtree have keys that are less than D's key and all the data items in D's right subtree have keys that are greater than D's key.

Operations

BSTree ()

Requirements:
None

Results:
Constructor. Creates an empty binary search tree.

~BSTree ()

Requirements:
None

Results:
Destructor. Deallocates (frees) the memory used to store a binary search tree.

void insert (const DT &newDataItem) throw (bad_alloc)

Requirements:
Binary search tree is not full.

Results:
Inserts newDataItem into a binary search tree. If a data item with the same key as newDataItem already exists in the tree, then updates that data item's nonkey fields with newDataItem's nonkey fields.

bool retrieve (KF searchKey, DT &searchDataItem) const

Requirements:
None

Results:
Searches a binary search tree for the data item with key searchKey. If this data item is found, then copies the data item to searchDataItem and returns true. Otherwise, returns false with searchDataItem undefined.

```
bool remove ( KF deleteKey )
```

Requirements:
None

Results:
Deletes the data item with key `deleteKey` from a binary search tree. If this data item is found, then deletes it from the tree and returns `true`. Otherwise, returns `false`.

```
void writeKeys () const
```

Requirements:
None

Results:
Outputs the keys of the data items in a binary search tree. The keys are output in ascending order, one per line.

```
void clear ()
```

Requirements:
None

Results:
Removes all the data items in a binary search tree.

```
bool isEmpty () const
```

Requirements:
None

Results:
Returns `true` if a binary search tree is empty. Otherwise, returns `false`.

```
bool isFull () const
```

Requirements:
None

Results:
Returns `true` if a binary search tree is full. Otherwise, returns `false`.

```
void showStructure () const
```

Requirements:
None

Results:
Outputs the keys in a binary search tree. The tree is output with its branches oriented from left (root) to right (leaves); that is, the tree is output rotated counterclockwise 90 degrees from its conventional orientation. If the tree is empty, outputs "Empty tree". Note that this operation is intended for debugging purposes only.

Laboratory 11: Cover Sheet

Name _____ Date _____

Section _____

Place a check mark in the *Assigned* column next to the exercises your instructor has assigned to you. Attach this cover sheet to the front of the packet of materials you submit following the laboratory.

Activities	Assigned: Check or list exercise numbers	Completed
Prelab Exercise		
Bridge Exercise		
In-lab Exercise 1		
In-lab Exercise 2		
In-lab Exercise 3		
Postlab Exercise 1		
Postlab Exercise 2		
Total		

Laboratory 11: Prelab Exercise

Name _____ Date _____

Section _____

Step 1: Implement the operations in Binary Search Tree ADT using a linked tree structure. As with the linear linked structures you developed in prior laboratories, your implementation of the linked tree structure uses a pair of classes: one for the nodes in the tree (BSTreeNode) and one for the overall tree structure (BSTree). Each node in the tree should contain a data item (dataItem) and a pair of pointers to the node's children (left and right). Your implementation should also maintain a pointer to the tree's root node (root). Base your implementation on the following declarations from the file *bstree.hs*. An implementation of the showStructure operation is given in the file *show11.cpp*.

```
template < class DT, class KF >
class BSTreeNode                    // Facilitator for the BSTree class
{
  private:

    // Constructor
    BSTreeNode ( const DT &nodeDataItem,
              BSTreeNode *leftPtr, BSTreeNode *rightPtr );

    // Data members
    DT dataItem;         // Binary search tree data item
    BSTreeNode *left,    // Pointer to the left child
            *right;    // Pointer to the right child

  friend class BSTree<DT,KF>;
};

template < class DT, class KF >    // DT : tree data item
class BSTree                       // KF : key field
{
  public:

    // Constructor
    BSTree ();

    // Destructor
    ~BSTree ();

    // Binary search tree manipulation operations
    void insert ( const DT &newDataItem )         // Insert data item
        throw ( bad_alloc );
    bool retrieve ( KF searchKey, DT &searchDataItem ) const;
                                                  // Retrieve data item
    bool remove ( KF deleteKey );                 // Remove data item
    void writeKeys () const;                      // Output keys
    void clear ();                                // Clear tree
```

```
    // Binary search tree status operations
    bool isEmpty () const;                      // Tree is empty
    bool isFull () const;                       // Tree is full

    // Output the tree structure -- used in testing/debugging
    void showStructure () const;

  private:

    // Recursive partners of the public member functions -- insert
    // prototypes of these functions here.
    void showSub ( BSTreeNode<DT,KF> *p, int level ) const;

    // Data member
    BSTreeNode<DT,KF> *root;    // Pointer to the root node
};
```

Step 2: The declaration of the BSTree class in the file *bstree.hs* does not include prototypes for the recursive private member functions needed by your implementation of the Binary Search Tree ADT. Add these prototypes and save the resulting class declarations in the file *bstree.h*.

Step 3: Save your implementation of the Binary Search Tree ADT in the file *bstree.cpp*. Be sure to document your code.

Laboratory 11: Bridge Exercise

Name _____   Date _____

Section _____

Check with your instructor whether you are to complete this exercise prior to your lab period or during lab.

The test program in the file *test11.cpp* allows you to interactively test your implementation of the Binary Search Tree ADT using the following commands.

Command	Action
+key	Insert (or update) the data item with the specified key.
?key	Retrieve the data item with the specified key and output it.
-key	Delete the data item with the specified key.
K	Output the keys in ascending order.
E	Report whether the tree is empty.
F	Report whether the tree is full.
C	Clear the tree.
Q	Quit the test program.

Step 1: Prepare a test plan for your implementation of the Binary Search Tree ADT. Your test plan should cover trees of various shapes and sizes, including empty, single branch, and single data item trees. A test plan form follows.

Step 2: Execute your test plan. If you discover mistakes in your implementation, correct them and execute your test plan again.

Test Plan for the Operations in the Binary Search Tree ADT

Test Case	Commands	Expected Result	Checked

Laboratory 11: In-lab Exercise 1

Name _____ Date _____

Section _____

A **database** is a collection of related pieces of information that is organized for easy retrieval. The following set of accounts records, for instance, form an accounts database.

Record #	Account ID	First name	Last name	Balance
0	6274	James	Johnson	415.56
1	2843	Marcus	Wilson	9217.23
2	4892	Maureen	Albright	51462.56
3	8337	Debra	Douglas	27.26
4	9523	Bruce	Gold	719.32
5	3165	John	Carlson	1496.24

Each record in the accounts database is assigned a record number based on that record's relative position within the database file. You can use a record number to retrieve an account record directly, much as you can use an array index to reference an array data item directly. The following program from the file *getdbrec.cpp*, for example, retrieves a record from the accounts database in the file *accounts.dat*.

```cpp
#include <iostream>
#include <fstream>

using namespace std;

//-------------------------------------------------------------
//
// Declarations specifying the accounts database
//

const int nameLength     = 11;   // Maximum number of characters in
                                 //    a name
const long bytesPerRecord = 38;  // Number of bytes used to store
                                 //    each record in the accounts
                                 //    database file

struct AccountRecord
{
    int acctID;                  // Account identifier
    char firstName[nameLength],  // Name of account holder
        lastName[nameLength];
    double balance;              // Account balance
};
```

Binary Search Tree ADT | 245

```
void main ()
{
    ifstream acctFile ("accounts.dat");   // Accounts database file
    AccountRecord acctRec;                // Account record
    long recNum;                          // User input record number

    // Get the record number to retrieve.

    cout << endl << "Enter record number: ";
    cin >> recNum;

    // Move to the corresponding record in the database file using the
    // seekg() function.

    acctFile.seekg(recNum*bytesPerRecord);

    // Read in the record.

    acctFile >> acctRec.acctID >> acctRec.firstName
            >> acctRec.lastName >> acctRec.balance;

    // Display the record.

    cout << recNum << " : " << acctRec.acctID << " "
        << acctRec.firstName << " " << acctRec.lastName << " "
        << acctRec.balance << endl;
}
```

Record numbers are assigned by the database file mechanism and are not part of the account information. As a result, they are not meaningful to database users. These users require a different record retrieval mechanism, one that is based on an account ID (the key for the database) rather than a record number.

Retrievals based on account ID require an index that associates each account ID with the corresponding record number. You can implement this index using a binary search tree in which each data item contains two fields: an account ID (the key) and a record number.

```
struct IndexEntry
{
    int acctID;                      // (Key) Account identifier
    long recNum;                     // Record number

    int getKey () const
        { return acctID; }           // Return key field
};

BSTree<IndexEntry,int> index;        // Database index
```

You build the index by reading through the database account by account, inserting successive (account ID, record number) pairs into the tree as you progress through the file. The following index tree, for instance, was produced by inserting the account records shown above into an (initially) empty tree.

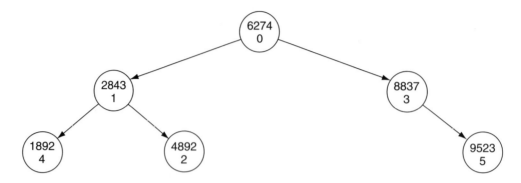

Given an account ID, retrieval of the corresponding account record is a two-step process. First, you retrieve the data item from the index tree that has the specified account ID. Then, using the record number stored in the index data item, you read the corresponding account record from the database file. The result is an efficient retrieval process that is based on account ID.

Step 1: Using the program shell given in the file *database.cs* as a basis, create a program that builds an index tree for the accounts database in the file *accounts.dat*. Once the index is built, your program should

- Output the account IDs in ascending order
- Read an account ID from the keyboard and output the corresponding account record

Step 2: Test your program using the accounts database in the text file *accounts.dat*. A copy of this database in given below. Try to retrieve several account IDs, including account IDs that do *not* occur in the database. A test plan form follows.

Record #	Account ID	First name	Last name	Balance
0	6274	James	Johnson	415.56
1	2843	Marcus	Wilson	9217.23
2	4892	Maureen	Albright	51462.56
3	8337	Debra	Douglas	27.26
4	9523	Bruce	Gold	719.32
5	3165	John	Carlson	1496.24
6	1892	Mary	Smith	918.26
7	3924	Simon	Becker	386.85
8	6023	John	Edgar	9.65
9	5290	George	Truman	16110.68
10	8529	Ellen	Fairchild	86.77
11	1144	Donald	Williams	4114.26

Test Plan for the Accounts Database Indexing Program

Test Case	Expected Result	Checked

Laboratory 11: In-lab Exercise 1

Name _____ Date _____

Section _____

Binary search trees containing the same data items can vary widely in shape depending on the order in which the data items were inserted into the trees. One measurement of a tree's shape is its **height**—that is, the number of nodes on the longest path from the root node to any leaf node. This statistic is significant because the amount of time that it can take to search for a data item in a binary search tree is a function of the height of the tree.

```
int getHeight () const;
```

Requirements:
None

Results:
Returns the height of a binary search tree.

You can compute the height of a binary search tree using a postorder traversal and the following recursive definition of height:

$$height(\text{p}) = \begin{cases} 0 & \text{if p} = 0 \text{ (base case)} \\ \max(height(\text{p} \rightarrow \text{left}),\ height(\text{p} \rightarrow \text{right})) + 1 & \text{if p} \neq 0 \text{ (recursive step)} \end{cases}$$

Step 1: Implement this operation and add it to the file *bstree.cpp*. A prototype for this operation is included in the declaration of the BSTree class in the file *bstree.h*.

Step 2: Activate the 'H' (height) command in the test program in the file *test11.cpp* by removing the comment delimiter (and the character 'H') from the lines that begin with "//H".

Step 3: Prepare a test plan for this operation that covers trees of various shapes and sizes, including empty and single-branch trees. A test plan form follows.

Step 4: Execute your test plan. If you discover mistakes in your implementation of the height operation, correct them and execute your test plan again.

Test Plan for the getHeight Operation

Test Case	Commands	Expected Result	Checked

Laboratory 11: In-lab Exercise 1

Name _____ Date _____

Section _____

You have created operations that retrieve a single data item from a binary search tree and output all the keys in a tree. The following operation outputs only those keys that are less than a specified key.

```
void writeLessThan ( KF searchKey ) const
```

Requirements:
None

Results:
Outputs the keys in a binary search tree that are less than `searchKey`. The keys are output in ascending order. Note that `searchKey` need not be a key in the tree.

You could implement this operation using an inorder traversal of the entire tree in which you compare each key with `searchKey` and output those that are less than `searchKey`. Although successful, this approach is inefficient. It searches subtrees that you know cannot possibly contain keys that are less than searchKey.

Suppose you are given a `searchKey` value of 37 and the following binary search tree:

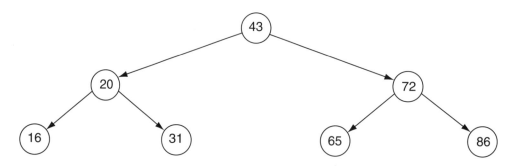

Because the root node contains the key 43, you can determine immediately that you do not need to search the root node's right subtree for keys that are less than 37. Similarly, if the value of `searchKey` were 67, then you would need to search the root node's right subtree but would not need to search the right subtree of the node whose key is 72. Your implementation of the `writeLessThan` operation should use this idea to limit the portion of the tree that must be searched.

Step 1: Implement this operation and add it to the file *bstree.cpp*. A prototype for this operation is included in the declaration of the BSTree class in the file *bstree.h*.

Step 2: Activate the '<' (less than) command in the test program in the file *test11.cpp* by removing the comment delimiter (and the character '<') from the lines that begin with "*//<*".

Step 3: Prepare a test plan for this operation that includes a variety of trees and values for `searchKey`, including values of `searchKey` that do *not* occur in a particular tree. Be sure to include test cases that limit searches to the left subtree of the root node, the left subtree and part of the right subtree of the root node, the leftmost branch in the tree, and the entire tree. A test plan form follows.

Step 4: Execute your test plan. If you discover mistakes in your implementation of the `writeLessThan` operation, correct them and execute your test plan again.

Test Plan for the `writeLessThan` Operation

Test Case	Commands	Expected Result	Checked

Laboratory 11: Postlab Exercise 1

Name _____   Date _____

Section _____

What are the heights of the shortest and tallest binary search trees that can be constructed from a set of N distinct keys? Give examples that illustrate your answer.

Laboratory 11: Postlab Exercise 2

Name _____ Date _____

Section _____

Given the shortest possible binary search tree containing N distinct keys, develop worst-case, order-of-magnitude estimates of the execution time of the following Binary Search Tree ADT operations. Briefly explain your reasoning behind each of your estimates.

retrieve	O( )
Explanation:	

insert	O( )
Explanation:	

remove   O(   )

Explanation:

writeKeys   O(   )

Explanation:

Expression Tree ADT

In this laboratory you will:

- Create an implementation of the Expression Tree ADT using a linked tree structure

- Develop an implementation of the Logic Expression Tree ADT and use your implementation to model a simple logic circuit

- Create an expression tree copy constructor

- Analyze how preorder, inorder, and postorder tree traversals are used in your implementation of the Expression Tree ADT

Overview

Although you ordinarily write arithmetic expressions in linear form, you treat them as hierarchical entities when you evaluate them. When evaluating the following arithmetic expression, for example,

(1+3)*(6-4)

you first add 1 and 3, then you subtract 4 from 6. Finally, you multiply these intermediate results together to produce the value of the expression. In performing these calculations, you have implicitly formed a hierarchy in which the multiply operator is built on a foundation consisting of the addition and subtraction operators. You can represent this hierarchy explicitly using the following binary tree. Trees such as this one are referred to as **expression trees.**

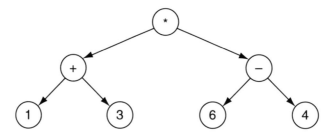

Expression Tree ADT

Data Items

Each node in an expression tree contains either an arithmetic operator or a numeric value.

Structure

The nodes form a tree in which each node containing an arithmetic operator has a pair of children. Each child is the root node of a subtree that represents one of the operator's operands. Nodes containing numeric values have no children.

Operations

ExprTree ()

Requirements:
None

Results:
Constructor. Creates an empty expression tree.

```
~ExprTree ()
```

Requirements:
None

Results:
Destructor. Deallocates (frees) the memory used to store an expression tree.

```
void build () throw ( bad_alloc )
```

Requirements:
None

Results:
Reads an arithmetic expression in prefix form from the keyboard and builds the corresponding expression tree.

```
void expression () const
```

Requirements:
None

Results:
Outputs the corresponding arithmetic expression in fully parenthesized infix form.

```
float evaluate () const throw ( logic_error )
```

Requirements:
Expression tree is not empty.

Results:
Returns the value of the corresponding arithmetic expression.

```
void clear ()
```

Requirements:
None

Results:
Removes all the data items in an expression tree.

```
void showStructure () const
```

Requirements:
Nonc

Results:
Outputs an expression tree with its branches oriented from left (root) to right (leaves)—that is, the tree is output rotated counterclockwise 90 degrees from its conventional orientation. If the tree is empty, outputs "Empty tree". Note that this operation is intended for testing/debugging purposes only. It assumes that arithmetic expressions contain only single-digit, nonnegative integers and the arithmetic operators for addition, subtraction, multiplication, and division.

We commonly write arithmetic expressions in **infix form**—that is, with each operator placed between its operands, as in the following expression:

(1 + 3) * (6 − 4)

In this laboratory, you construct an expression tree from the **prefix form** of an arithmetic expression. In prefix form, each operator is placed immediately before its operands. The expression above is written in prefix form as

* + 1 3 − 6 4

When processing the prefix form of an arithmetic expression from left to right, you will, by definition, encounter each operator followed by its operands. If you know in advance the number of operands an operator has, you can use the following recursive process to construct the corresponding expression tree.

Read the next arithmetic operator or numeric value.

Create a node containing the operator or numeric value.

if the node contains an operator

then Recursively build the subtrees that correspond to the

operator's operands.

else The node is a leaf node.

If you apply this process to the arithmetic expression

* + 1 3 − 6 4

then construction of the corresponding expression tree proceeds as follows:

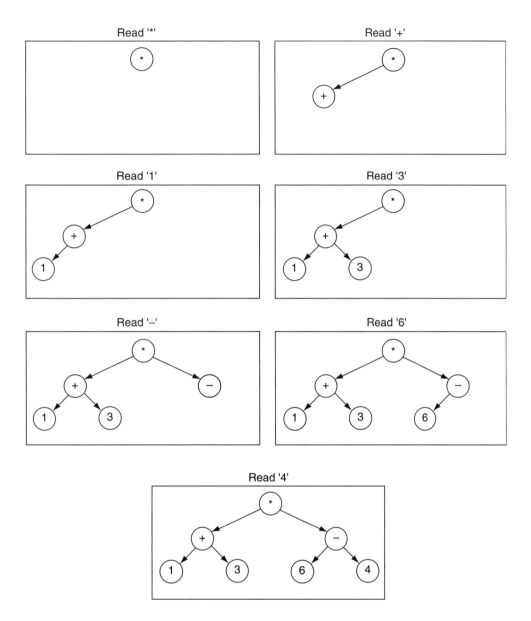

Note that in processing this arithmetic expression we have assumed that all numeric values are single-digit, nonnegative integers, and thus, that all numeric values can be represented as a single character. If we were to generalize this process to include multidigit numbers, we would have to include delimiters in the expression to separate numbers.

Laboratory 12: Cover Sheet

Name _____   Date _____

Section _____

Place a check mark in the *Assigned* column next to the exercises your instructor has assigned to you. Attach this cover sheet to the front of the packet of materials you submit following the laboratory.

Activities	Assigned: Check or list exercise numbers	Completed
Prelab Exercise		
Bridge Exercise		
In-lab Exercise 1		
In-lab Exercise 2		
In-lab Exercise 3		
Postlab Exercise 1		
Postlab Exercise 2		
Total		

Laboratory 12: Prelab Exercise

Name _____ Date _____

Section _____

In the Overview you saw how the construction of an expression tree can be described using recursion. In this exercise you will use recursive functions to implement the operations in the Expression Tree ADT.

Step 1: Implement the operations in Expression Tree ADT using a linked tree structure. Assume that an arithmetic expression consists of single-digit, nonnegative integers ('0'..'9') and the four basic arithmetic operators ('+', '-', '*', and '/'). Further assume that each arithmetic expression is input in prefix form from the keyboard with all of the characters on one line.

As with the linear linked structures you developed in prior laboratories, your implementation of the linked tree structure uses a pair of classes: one for the nodes in the tree (ExprTreeNode) and one for the overall tree structure (ExprTree). Each node in the tree should contain a character (dataItem) and a pair of pointers to the node's children (left and right). Your implementation also should maintain a pointer to the tree's root node (root). Base your implementation on the following declarations from the file *exprtree.hs*. An implementation of the showStructure operation is given in the file *show12.cpp*.

```
class ExprTree;          // Forward declaration of the ExprTree class

class ExprTreeNode        // Facilitator class for the ExprTree class
{
  private:

    // Constructor
    ExprTreeNode ( char elem,
                   ExprTreeNode *leftPtr, ExprTreeNode *rightPtr );

    // Data members
    char dataItem;        // Expression tree data item
    ExprTreeNode *left,   // Pointer to the left child
                 *right;  // Pointer to the right child

  friend class ExprTree;
};
```

```
//-------------------------------------------------------------------

class ExprTree
{
  public:

    // Constructor
    ExprTree ();

    // Destructor
    ~ExprTree ();

    // Expression tree manipulation operations
    void build ()                  // Build tree from prefix expression
        throw ( bad_alloc );
    void expression () const;     // Output expression in infix form
    float evaluate () const       // Evaluate expression
        throw ( logic_error );
    void clear ();                 // Clear tree

    // Output the tree structure -- used in testing/debugging
    void showStructure () const;

  private:

    // Recursive partners of the public member functions -- insert
    // prototypes of these functions here.
    void showSub ( ExprTreeNode *p, int level ) const;

    // Data member
    ExprTreeNode *root;    // Pointer to the root node
};
```

Step 2: The declaration of the ExprTree class in the file *exprtree.hs* does not include prototypes for the recursive private member functions needed by your implementation of the Expression Tree ADT. Add these prototypes and save the resulting class declarations in the file *exprtree.h*.

Step 3: Save your implementation of the Expression Tree ADT in the file *exprtree.cpp*. Be sure to document your code.

Laboratory 12: Bridge Exercise

Name _____ Date _____

Section _____

Check with your instructor whether you are to complete this exercise prior to your lab period or during lab.

Test your implementation of the Expression Tree ADT using the test program in the file *test12.cpp*.

Step 1: Compile your implementation of the Expression Tree ADT in the file *exprtree.cpp*.

Step 2: Compile the test program in the file *test12.cpp*.

Step 3: Link the object files produced by Steps 1 and 2.

Step 4: Complete the following test plan by filling in the expected result for each arithmetic expression. You may wish to add arithmetic expressions to the test plan.

Step 5: Execute this test plan. If you discover mistakes in your implementation of the Expression Tree ADT, correct them and execute the test plan again.

Test Plan for the Operations in the Expression Tree ADT

Test Case	Arithmetic Expression	Expected Result	Checked
One operator	+34		
Nested operators	*+34/52		
All operators at start	-/*9321		
Uneven nesting	*4+6-75		
Zero dividend	/02		
Single-digit number	7		

Laboratory 12: In-lab Exercise 1

Name _____ Date _____

Section _____

Computers are composed of logic circuits that take a set of Boolean input values and produce a Boolean output. You can represent this mapping from inputs to output with a logic expression consisting of the Boolean logic operators AND, OR, and NOT (defined below) and the Boolean values True (1) and False (0).

	(NOT)			(AND)	(OR)
A	-A	A	B	A*B	A+B
0	1	0	0	0	0
1	0	0	1	0	1
		1	0	0	1
		1	1	1	1

Just as you can construct an arithmetic expression tree from an arithmetic expression, you can construct a logic expression tree from a logic expression. For example, the following logic expression:

`(1*0)+(1*-0)`

can be expressed in prefix form as

`+*10*1-0`

Applying the expression tree construction process described in the overview to this expression produces the following logic expression tree.

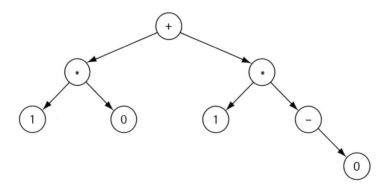

Evaluating this tree yields the Boolean value True (1).

Construction of this tree requires processing a unary operator, the Boolean operator NOT ('-'). When building a logic expression tree, we will choose to set the right child of any node containing the NOT operator to point to the operand and set the left child to null. Note that you must be careful when performing the remaining operations to avoid traversing these null left children.

Step 1: Modify the prototype of the `evaluate()` function in the file *exprtree.h* so that this function yields an integer value rather than a floating-point number. You may also need to modify the prototype of a related recursive private member function. Save the resulting class declarations in the file *logitree.h*.

Step 2: Create an implementation of the Expression Tree ADT that supports logic expressions consisting of the Boolean values True and False ('1' and '0') and the Boolean operators AND, OR, and NOT ('*', '+', and '-'). Base your implementation on the declarations in the file *logitree.h*. Save your implementation of the Logic Expression Tree ADT in the file *logitree.cpp*.

Step 3: Modify the test program in the file *test12.cpp* so that the header file for the Logic Expression Tree ADT (*logitree.h*) is included in place of the header file for the (arithmetic) Expression Tree ADT.

Step 4: Compile and link your implementation of the Logic Expression Tree ADT and the modified test program.

Step 5: Complete the following test plan by filling in the expected result for each logic expression. You may wish to include additional logic expressions in this test plan.

Step 6: Execute this test plan. If you discover mistakes in your implementation of the Logic Expression Tree ADT, correct them and execute the test plan again.

Test Plan for the Operations in the Logic Expression Tree ADT

Test Case	Logic Expression	Expected Result	Checked
One operator	+10		
Nested operators	*+10+01		
NOT (Boolean value)	+*10*1-0		
NOT (subexpression)	+-1-*11		
NOT (nested expression)	-*+110		
Double negation	--1		
Boolean value	1		

Having produced a tool that constructs and evaluates logic expression trees, you can use this tool to investigate the use of logic circuits to perform binary arithmetic. Suppose you have two one-bit binary numbers (X and Y). You can add these numbers together to produce a one-bit sum (S) and a one-bit carry (C). The results of one-bit binary addition for all combinations of X and Y are tabulated below.

	X	Y	C	S
X	0	0	0	0
+ Y	0	1	0	1
C S	1	0	0	1
	1	1	1	0

A brief analysis of this table reveals that you can compute the values of outputs S and C from inputs X and Y using the following pair of (prefix) logic expressions.

C = *XY   S = +*X-Y*-XY

Step 7: Using your implementation of the Logic Expression Tree ADT and the modified test program, confirm that these expressions are correct by completing the following table.

X	Y	C = *XY	S = +*X-Y*-XY
0	0	*00 =	+*0-0*-00 =
0	1	*01 =	+*0-1*-01 =
1	0	*10 =	+*1-0*-10 =
1	1	*11 =	+*1-1*-11 =

Laboratory 12: In-lab Exercise 2

Name _____   Date _____

Section _____

In Laboratory 8 you created a copy constructor for a data structure that was represented using a linked list. In this exercise, you create a copy constructor for your linked tree implementation of the Expression Tree ADT.

```
ExprTree ( const ExprTree &valueTree )
```

Requirements:
None

Results:
Copy constructor. Creates a copy of `valueTree`. This constructor is automatically invoked whenever an expression tree is passed to a function using call by value, a function returns an expression tree, or an expression tree is initialized using another expression tree.

Step 1: Implement this operation and add it to the file *exprtree.cpp*. A prototype for this operation is included in the declaration of the ExprTree class in the file *exprtree.h*.

Step 2: Activate the test for the copy constructor in the test program in the file *test12.cpp* by removing the comment delimiter (and the character '2') from the lines that begin with "//2".

Step 3: Prepare a test plan for this operation that includes a variety of expression trees, including empty trees and trees containing a single data item. A test plan form follows.

Step 4: Execute your test plan. If you discover mistakes in your implementation of the copy constructor, correct them and execute the test plan again.

Test Plan for the Copy Constructor

Test Case	Arithmetic Expression	Expected Result	Checked

Laboratory 12: In-lab Exercise 1

Name _____   Date _____

Section _____

You no doubt remember the **commutative property** in mathematics. It guarantees, for instance, that a+b = b+a. Swapping the + operator's operands results in an expression that has the same value. The commutative property is not true for all operators—a/b is generally not equal to b/a— but the operands of all binary operators can be **commuted** (swapped). Commuting the operators in an arithmetic expression requires restructuring the nodes in the corresponding expression tree. For example, commuting *every* operator in the expression tree

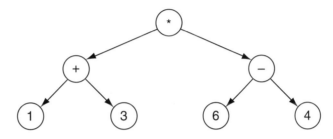

yields the expression tree

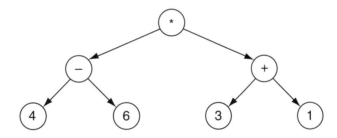

An operation for commuting expression trees is described below.

```
void commute ()
```

Requirements:
None

Results:
Commutes the operands for every arithmetic operator in an expression tree.

Step 1: Implement this operation and add it to the file *exprtree.cpp*. A prototype for this operation is included in the declaration of the ExprTree class in the file *exprtree.h*.

Step 2: Activate the test for the commute operation in the test program in the file *test12.cpp* by removing the comment delimiter (and the character '3') from the lines that begin with "//3".

Step 3: Prepare a test plan for this operation that includes a variety of arithmetic expressions. A test plan form follows.

Step 4: Execute your test plan. If you discover mistakes in your implementation of the commute operation, correct them and execute the test plan again.

Test Plan for the Commute Operation

Test Case	Arithmetic Expression	Expected Result	Checked

Laboratory 12: Postlab Exercise 1

Name _____ Date _____

Section _____

What type of tree traversal (inorder, preorder, or postorder) serves as the basis of your implementation of each of the following Expression Tree ADT operations? Briefly explain why you used a given traversal to implement a particular operation.

<table>
<tr><td align="center">build</td></tr>
<tr><td>Traversal:</td></tr>
<tr><td>Explanation:</td></tr>
</table>

<table>
<tr><td align="center">expression</td></tr>
<tr><td>Traversal:</td></tr>
<tr><td>Explanation:</td></tr>
</table>

evaluate

Traversal:

Explanation:

clear

Traversal:

Explanation:

Laboratory 12: Postlab Exercise 2

Name _____ Date _____

Section _____

Consider the functions `writeSub1()` and `writeSub2()` given below:

```
void writeSub1 ( ExprTreeNode *p ) const
{
    if ( p != 0 )
    {
        writeSub1(p->left);
        cout << p->dataItem;
        writeSub1(p->right);
    }
}

void writeSub2 ( ExprTreeNode *p ) const
{
    if ( p->left != 0 ) writeSub2(p->left);
    cout << p->dataItem;
    if ( p->right != 0 ) writeSub2(p->right);
}
```

Let `root` be the pointer to the root node of a nonempty expression tree. Will the following pair of function calls produce the same output?

```
writeSub1(root); and writeSub2(root);
```

If not, why not? If so, how do the functions differ and why might this difference be important?

Weighted Graph ADT

In this laboratory you will:

- Create an implementation of the Weighted Graph ADT using a vertex list and an adjacency matrix

- Develop a routine that finds the least costly (or shortest) path between each pair of vertices in a graph

- Add vertex coloring and implement a function that checks whether a graph has a proper coloring

- Investigate the Four-Color Theorem by generating a graph for which no proper coloring can be created using less than five colors

Objectives

Overview

Many relationships cannot be expressed easily using either a linear or a hierarchical data structure. The relationship between the cities connected by a highway network is one such relationship. Although it is possible for the roads in the highway network to describe a relationship between cities that is either linear (a one-way street, for example) or hierarchical (an expressway and its off ramps, for instance), we all have driven in circles enough times to know that most highway networks are neither linear nor hierarchical. What we need is a data structure that lets us connect each city to any of the other cities in the network. This type of data structure is referred to as a **graph**.

Like a tree, a graph consists of a set of nodes (called vertices) and a set of edges. Unlike a tree, an edge in a graph can connect any pair of vertices, not simply a parent and its child. The following graph represents a simple highway network.

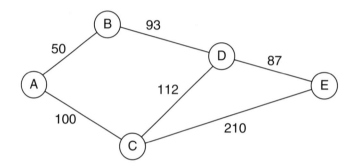

Each vertex in the graph has a unique **label** that denotes a particular city. Each edge has a **weight** that denotes the cost (measured in terms of distance, time, or money) of traversing the corresponding road. Note that the edges in the graph are **undirected**; that is, if there is an edge connecting a pair of vertices A and B, this edge can be used to move either from A to B or from B to A. The resulting **weighted, undirected graph** expresses the cost of traveling between cities using the roads in the highway network. In this laboratory, you focus on the implementation and application of weighted, undirected graphs.

Weighted Graph ADT

Data Items

Each vertex in a graph has a label (of type `char*`) that uniquely identifies it. Vertices may include additional data.

Structure

The relationship between the vertices in a graph is expressed using a set of undirected edges, where each edge connects one pair of vertices. Collectively, these edges define a symmetric relation between the vertices. Each edge in a weighted graph has a weight that denotes the cost of traversing that edge.

Operations

```
WtGraph ( int maxNumber = defMaxGraphSize )
     throw ( bad_alloc )
```

Requirements:
None

Results:
Constructor. Creates an empty graph. Allocates enough memory for a graph containing `maxNumber` vertices.

```
~WtGraph ()
```

Requirements:
None

Results:
Destructor. Deallocates (frees) the memory used to store a graph.

```
void insertVertex ( Vertex newVertex ) throw ( logic_error )
```

Requirements:
Graph is not full.

Results:
Inserts `newVertex` into a graph. If the vertex already exists in the graph, then updates it.

```
void insertEdge ( char *v1, char *v2, int wt )
     throw ( logic_error )
```

Requirements:
Graph includes vertices v1 and v2.

Results:
Inserts an undirected edge connecting vertices v1 and v2 into a graph. The weight of the edge is `wt`. If there is already an edge connecting these vertices, then updates the weight of the edge.

```
bool retrieveVertex ( char *v, Vertex &vData ) const
```

Requirements:
None

Results:
Searches a graph for vertex v. If this vertex is found, then copies the vertex's data to `vData` and returns `true`. Otherwise, returns `false` with `vData` undefined.

```
bool getEdgeWeight ( char *v1, char *v2, int &wt ) const
    throw ( logic_error )
```

Requirements:
Graph includes vertices v1 and v2.

Results:
Searches a graph for the edge connecting vertices v1 and v2. If this edge exists, then returns true with wt returning the weight of the edge. Otherwise, returns false with wt undefined.

```
void removeVertex ( char *v ) throw ( logic_error )
```

Requirements:
Graph includes vertex v.

Results:
Removes vertex v from a graph.

```
void removeEdge ( char *v1, char *v2 ) throw ( logic_error )
```

Requirements:
Graph includes vertices v1 and v2.

Results:
Removes the edge connecting vertices v1 and v2 from a graph.

```
void clear ()
```

Requirements:
None

Results:
Removes all the vertices and edges in a graph.

```
bool isEmpty () const
```

Requirements:
None

Results:
Returns true if a graph is empty (no vertices). Otherwise, returns false.

```
bool isFull () const
```

Requirements:
None

Results:
Returns true if a graph is full. Otherwise, returns false.

```
void showStructure () const
```

Requirements:
None

Results:
Outputs a graph with the vertices in array form and the edges in adjacency matrix form (with their weights). If the graph is empty, outputs "Empty graph". Note that this operation is intended for testing/debugging purposes only.

Laboratory 13: Cover Sheet

Name _____ Date _____

Section _____

Place a check mark in the *Assigned* column next to the exercises your instructor has assigned to you. Attach this cover sheet to the front of the packet of materials you submit following the laboratory.

Activities	Assigned: Check or list exercise numbers	Completed
Prelab Exercise		
Bridge Exercise		
In-lab Exercise 1		
In-lab Exercise 2		
In-lab Exercise 3		
Postlab Exercise 1		
Postlab Exercise 2		
Total		

Laboratory 13: Prelab Exercise

Name _____ Date _____

Section _____

You can represent a graph in many ways. In this laboratory you will use an array to store the set of vertices and an **adjacency matrix** to store the set of edges. An entry (j,k) in an adjacency matrix contains information on the edge that goes from the vertex with index j to the vertex with index k. For a weighted graph, each matrix entry contains the weight of the corresponding edge. A specially chosen weight value is used to indicate edges that are missing from the graph.

The following graph yields the vertex list and adjacency matrix shown below. A '–' is used to denote an edge that is missing from the graph.

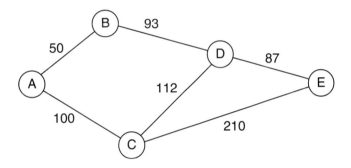

Vertex list		Adjacency matrix					
Index	Label	From\To	0	1	2	3	4
0	A	0	–	50	100	–	–
1	B	1	50	–	–	93	–
2	C	2	100	–	–	112	210
3	D	3	–	93	112	–	87
4	E	4	–	–	210	87	–

Vertex A has an array index of 0 and vertex C has an array index of 2. The weight of the edge from vertex A to vertex C is therefore stored in entry (0,2) in the adjacency matrix.

Step 1: Implement the operations in the Weighted Graph ADT using an array to store the vertices (vertexList) and an adjacency matrix to store the edges (adjMatrix). The number of vertices in a graph is not fixed; therefore, you need to store the maximum number of vertices the graph can hold (maxSize) as well as the actual number of vertices in the graph (size). Base your implementation on the following declarations from the file *wtgraph.h*. An implementation of the showStructure operation is given in the file *show13.cpp*.

```
const int defMaxGraphSize = 10,        // Default number of vertices
          vertexLabelLength = 11,      // Length of a vertex label
          infiniteEdgeWt = INT_MAX;    // "Weight" of a missing edge

class Vertex
{
  public:

    char label [vertexLabelLength];    // Vertex label
};

class WtGraph
{
  public:

    // Constructor
    WtGraph ( int maxNumber = defMaxGraphSize )
        throw ( bad_alloc );

    // Destructor
    ~WtGraph ();

    // Graph manipulation operations
    void insertVertex ( Vertex newVertex )            // Insert vertex
        throw ( logic_error );
    void insertEdge ( char *v1, char *v2, int wt )    // Insert edge
        throw ( logic_error );
    bool retrieveVertex ( char *v, Vertex &vData );
                                                      // Get vertex
    bool getEdgeWeight ( char *v1, char *v2, int &wt )
        throw ( logic_error );                        // Get edge wt.
    void removeVertex ( char *v )                     // Remove vertex
        throw ( logic_error );
    void removeEdge ( char *v1, char *v2 )            // Remove edge
        throw ( logic_error );
    void clear ();                                    // Clear graph

    // Graph status operations
    bool isEmpty () const;                            // Graph is empty
    bool isFull () const;                             // Graph is full

    // Output the graph structure — used in testing/debugging
    void showStructure ();

  private:

    // Facilitator functions
    int getIndex ( char *v );                 // Converts vertex label to
                                              // an adjacency matrix
                                              // index

    int getEdge ( int row, int col );         // Get edge weight using
    void setEdge ( int row, int col, int wt); // Set edge weight using
                                              // adjacency matrix
                                              // indices
```

```
    // Data members
    int maxSize,          // Maximum number of vertices in the graph
        size;             // Actual number of vertices in the graph
    Vertex *vertexList;   // Vertex list
    int *adjMatrix;       // Adjacency matrix
};
```

Your implementations of the public member functions should use your `getEdge()` and `setEdge()` facilitator functions to access entries in the adjacency matrix. For example, the assignment statement

```
setEdge(2,3, 100);
```

uses the `setEdge()` function to assign a weight of 100 to the entry in the second row, third column of the adjacency matrix. The `if` statement

```
if ( getEdge(j,k) == infiniteEdgeWt )
    cout << "Edge is missing from graph" << endl;
```

uses this function to test whether there is an edge connecting the vertex with index `j` and the vertex with index `k`.

Step 2: Save your implementation of the Weighted Graph ADT in the file *wtgraph.cpp*. Be sure to document your code.

Laboratory 13: Bridge Exercise

Name _____ Date _____

Section _____

Check with your instructor whether you are to complete this exercise prior to your lab period or during lab.

The test program in the file *test13.cpp* allows you to interactively test your implementation of the Weighted Graph ADT using the following commands.

Command	Action
+v	Insert vertex v.
=v w wt	Insert an edge connecting vertices v and w. The weight of this edge is wt.
?v	Retrieve vertex v.
#v w	Retrieve the edge connecting vertices v and w and output its weight.
-v	Remove vertex v.
!v w	Remove the edge connecting vertices v and w.
E	Report whether the graph is empty.
F	Report whether the graph is full.
C	Clear the graph.
Q	Quit the test program.

Note that v and w denote vertex labels (type char*), not individual characters (type char). As a result, you must be careful to enter these commands using the exact format shown above—including spaces.

Step 1: Prepare a test plan for your implementation of the Weighted Graph ADT. Your test plan should cover graphs in which the vertices are connected in a variety of ways. Be sure to include test cases that attempt to retrieve edges that do not exist or that connect nonexistent vertices. A test plan form follows.

Step 2: Execute your test plan. If you discover mistakes in your implementation, correct them and execute your test plan again.

Test Plan for the Operations in the Weighted Graph ADT

Test Case	Commands	Expected Result	Checked

Laboratory 13: In-lab Exercise 1

Name _____ Date _____

Section _____

In many applications of weighted graphs, you need to determine not only whether there is an edge connecting a pair of vertices, but whether there is a path connecting the vertices. By extending the concept of an adjacency matrix, you can produce a **path matrix** in which an entry (j,k) contains the cost of the least costly (or **shortest**) path from the vertex with index j to the vertex with index k. The following graph yields the path matrix shown below.

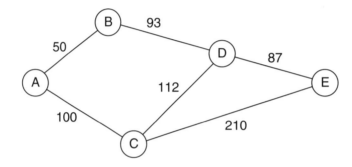

Vertex list		Path matrix					
Index	Label	From/To:	0	1	2	3	4
0	A	0	0	50	100	143	230
1	B	1	50	0	150	93	180
2	C	2	100	150	0	112	199
3	D	3	143	93	112	0	87
4	E	4	230	180	199	87	0

This graph includes a number of paths from vertex A to vertex E. The cost of the least costly path connecting these vertices is stored in entry (0,4) in the path matrix, where 0 is the index of vertex A and 4 is the index of vertex E. The corresponding path is ABDE.

In creating this path matrix, we have assumed that a path with cost 0 exists from a vertex to itself (entries of the form (j, j)). This assumption is based on the view that traveling from a vertex to itself is a nonevent and thus costs nothing. Depending on how you intend to apply the information in a graph, you may want to use an alternative assumption.

Given the adjacency matrix for a graph, we begin construction of the path matrix by noting that all edges are paths. These one-edge-long paths are combined to form two-edge-long paths by applying the following reasoning.

> If   there exists a path from a vertex j to a vertex m and
>   there exists a path from a vertex m to a vertex k,
> then   there exists a path from vertex j to vertex k.

We can apply this same reasoning to these newly generated paths to form paths consisting of more and more edges. The key to this process is to enumerate and combine paths in a manner that is both complete and efficient. One approach to this task is described in the following algorithm, known as Warshall's algorithm. Note that variables j, k, and m refer to vertex indices, *not* vertex labels.

```
Initialize the path matrix so that it is the same as the edge
matrix (all edges are paths). In addition, create a path with
cost 0 from each vertex back to itself.

for ( m = 0 ; m < size ; m++ )
  for ( j = 0 ; j < size ; j++ )
    for ( k = 0 ; k < size ; k++ )
        If there exists a path from vertex j to vertex m and
            there exists a path from vertex m to vertex k,
        then add a path from vertex j to vertex k to the path matrix.
```

This algorithm establishes the existence of paths between vertices but not their costs. Fortunately, by extending the reasoning used above, we can easily determine the costs of the least costly paths between vertices.

```
If there exists a path from a vertex j to a vertex m and
   there exists a path from a vertex m to a vertex k and
   the cost of going from j to m to k is less than entry (j,k) in
      the path matrix,
then replace entry (j,k) with the sum of entries (j,m) and (m,k).
```

Incorporating this reasoning into the previous algorithm yields the following algorithm, known as Floyd's algorithm.

```
Initialize the path matrix so that it is the same as the edge
matrix (all edges are paths). In addition, create a path with
cost 0 from each vertex back to itself.

for ( m = 0 ; m < size ; m++ )
  for ( j = 0 ; j < size ; j++ )
    for ( k = 0 ; k < size ; k++ )
        If there exists a path from vertex j to vertex m and
            there exists a path from vertex m to vertex k and
                the sum of entries (j,m) and (m,k) is less than entry
                    (j,k) in the path matrix,
        then replace entry (j,k) with the sum of entries (j,m)
                and (m,k).
```

The following Weighted Graph ADT operation computes a graph's path matrix.

```
void computePaths ()
```

Requirements:
None

Results:
Computes a graph's path matrix.

Step 1: Add the data member

```
int *pathMatrix;    // Path matrix
```

and the function prototype

```
void computePaths ();    // Computes path matrix
```

to the WtGraph class declaration in the file *wtgraph.h.*

Step 2: Implement the `computePaths` operation described above and add it to the file *wtgraph.cpp.*

Step 3: Replace the `showStructure()` function in the file *wtgraph.cpp* with a `showStructure()` function that outputs a graph's path matrix in addition to its vertex list and adjacency matrix. An implementation of this function is given in the file *show14.cpp.*

Step 4: Activate the "PM" (path matrix) test in the test program *test13.cpp* by removing the comment delimiter (and the characters "PM") from the lines that begin with "//PM".

Step 5: Prepare a test plan for the `computePaths` operation that includes graphs in which the vertices are connected in a variety of ways with a variety of weights. Be sure to include test cases in which an edge between a pair of vertices has a higher cost than a multiedge path between these same vertices. The edge CE and the path CDE in the graph shown earlier have this property. A test plan form follows.

Step 6: Execute your test plan. If you discover mistakes in your implementation of the `computePaths` operation, correct them and execute your test plan again.

Test Plan for the `computePaths` Operation

Test Case	Commands	Expected Result	Checked

Laboratory 13: In-lab Exercise 2

Name _____   Date _____

Section _____

Suppose you wish to create a road map of a particular highway network. To avoid causing confusion among map users, you must be careful to color the cities in such a way that no cities sharing a common border also share the same color. An assignment of colors to cities that meets this criterion is called a **proper coloring** of the map.

Restating this problem in terms of a graph, we say that an assignment of colors to the vertices in a graph is a proper coloring of the graph if no vertex is assigned the same color as an adjacent vertex. The assignment of colors (gray and white) shown in the following graph is an example of a proper coloring.

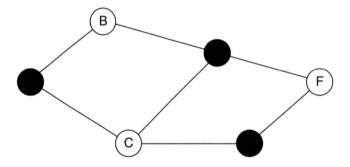

Two colors are not always enough to produce a proper coloring. One of the most famous theorems in graph theory, the Four-Color Theorem, states that creating a proper coloring of any **planar graph** (that is, any graph that can be drawn on a sheet of paper without having the edges cross one another) requires using at most four colors. A planar graph that requires four colors is shown below. Note that if a graph is not planar, you may need to use more than four colors.

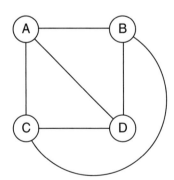

The following Weighted Graph ADT operation determines whether a graph has a proper coloring.

```
bool hasProperColoring () const
```

Requirements:
All the vertices have been assigned a color.

Results:
Returns `true` if no vertex in a graph has the same color as an adjacent vertex. Otherwise, returns `false`.

Step 1: Add the following data member to the `Vertex` class declaration in the file *wtgraph.h.*

```
char color;   // Vertex color ('r' for red and so forth)
```

Add the following function prototype to the `WtGraph` class declaration in the file *wtgraph.h.*

```
bool hasProperColoring () const;   // Proper coloring?
```

Step 2: Implement the `hasProperColoring` operation described above and add it to the file *wtgraph.cpp.*

Step 3: Replace the `showStructure()` function in the file *wtgraph.cpp* with a `showStructure()` function that outputs a vertex's color in addition to its label. An implementation of this function is given in the file *show13.cpp.*

Step 4: Activate the "P" (proper coloring) command in the test program *test13.cpp* by removing the comment delimiter (and the characters "PC") from the lines that begin with "//PC".

Step 5: Prepare a test plan for the `properColoring` operation that includes a variety of graphs and vertex colorings. A test plan form follows.

Step 6: Execute your test plan. If you discover mistakes in your implementation of the `properColoring` operation, correct them and execute your test plan again.

Test Plan for the `properColoring` **Operation**

Test Case	Commands	Expected Result	Checked

Laboratory 13: In-lab Exercise 3

Name _____ Date _____

Section _____

A communications network consists of a set of switching centers (vertices) and a set of communications lines (edges) that connect these centers. When designing a network, a communications company needs to know whether the resulting network will continue to support communications between *all* centers should one of these communications lines be rendered inoperative due to weather or equipment failure. That is, they need to know the answer to the following question.

Given a graph in which there is a path from every vertex to every other vertex, will removing any edge from the graph always produce a graph in which there is *still* a path from every vertex to every other vertex?

Obviously, the answer to this question depends on the graph. The answer for the graph shown below is yes.

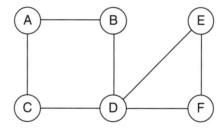

On the other hand, you can divide the following graph into two disconnected subgraphs by removing the edge connecting vertices D and E. Thus, for this graph the answer is no.

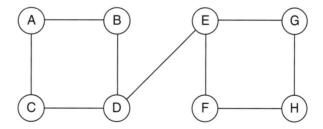

Although determining an answer to this question for an arbitrary graph is somewhat difficult, there are certain classes of graphs for which the answer is always yes. Given the definitions:

- A graph G is said to be **connected** if there exists a path from every vertex in G to every other vertex in G.
- The **degree** of a vertex V in a graph G is the number of edges in G which connect to V, where an edge from V to itself counts twice.

The following rule can be derived using simple graph theory:

If all of the vertices in a connected graph are of even degree, then removing any one edge from the graph will always produce a connected graph.

If this rule applies to a graph, then you know that the answer to the previous question is yes for that graph. Note that this rule tells you nothing about connected graphs in which the degree of one or more vertices is odd.

The following Weighted Graph ADT operation checks whether every vertex in a graph is of even degree.

```
bool areAllEven () const
```

Requirements:
None

Results:
Returns `true` if every vertex in a graph is of even degree. Otherwise, returns `false`.

Step 1: Implement the `areAllEven` operation described above and add it to the file *wtgraph.cpp*. A prototype for this operation is included in the declaration of the `WtGraph` class in the file *wtgraph.h*.

Step 2: Activate the 'D' (degree) command in the test program *test13.cpp* by removing the comment delimiter (and the character 'D') from the lines that begin with "//D".

Step 3: Prepare a test plan for this operation that includes graphs in which the vertices are connected in a variety of ways. A test plan form follows.

Step 4: Execute your test plan. If you discover mistakes in your implementation of the `areAllEven` operation, correct them and execute your test plan again.

Test Plan for the `areAllEven` Operation

Test Case	Commands	Expected Result	Checked

Laboratory 13: Postlab Exercise 1

Name _____ Date _____

Section _____

Floyd's algorithm (In-lab Exercise 1) computes the shortest path between each pair of vertices in a graph. Suppose you need to know not only the cost of the shortest path between a pair of vertices, but also which vertices lie along this path. At first, it may seem that you need to store a list of vertices for every entry in the path matrix. Fortunately, you do not need to store this much information. For each entry (j,k) in the path matrix, all you need to know is the index of the vertex that follows j on the shortest path from j to k—that is, the index of the second vertex on the shortest path from j to k. The following graph, for example,

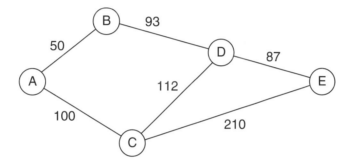

yields the augmented path matrix shown below.

Vertex list		Path matrix (cost|second vertex on shortest path)				
Index	Label	From/To	0	1	2	3	4
0	A	0	0|0	50|1	100|2	143|1	230|1
1	B	1	50|0	0|1	150|0	93|3	180|3
2	C	2	100|0	150|0	0|2	112|3	199|3
3	D	3	143|1	93|1	112|2	0|3	87|4
4	E	4	230|3	180|3	199|3	87|3	0|4

Entry (0,4) in this path matrix indicates that the cost of the shortest path from vertex A to vertex E is 230. It further indicates that vertex B (the vertex with index 1) is the second vertex on the shortest path. Thus the shortest path is of the form AB . . . E.

Explain how you can use this augmented path matrix to list the vertices that lie along the shortest path between a given pair of vertices.

Laboratory 13: Postlab Exercise 2

Name _____   Date _____

Section _____

Give an example of a graph for which no proper coloring can be created using less than five colors (see In-lab Exercise 2). Does your example contradict the Four-Color Theorem?

Hash Table ADT

In this laboratory you will:

- Implement the Hash Table ADT using an array of lists representation

- Use a hash table to implement a password-based authentication system

- Implement a perfect hash to store selected C++ reserved words

- Implement a standard deviation analysis operation to analyze the uniformity of the key distribution

- Analyze the efficiency of your implementation of the Hash Table ADT

Objectives

Overview

The data structures you have implemented up to this point are all useful and widely used. However, their average performance for insertion and retrieval is generally $O(N)$, or at best $O(\log_2 N)$. As N becomes large—*large* is a relative term, depending on current hardware configuration and performance, data record size and a number of other factors, but let's say hundreds of thousands or millions of records—$O(N)$ becomes a poor choice. Even $O(\log_2 N)$ performance can be unacceptable when handling many simultaneous queries or processing large reports. How does searching, inserting, and retrieving in $O(1)$ sound? That is the possibility that the Hash Table ADT tries to offer. Hash tables are among the fastest data structures for most operations and come closest to offering $O(1)$ performance. Consequently, a hash table is the preferred data structure in many contexts. For instance, most electronic library catalogs are based on hash tables.

The goal of the ideal hash table is to come up with a unique mapping of each key onto a specific location in an array. The mapping of the key to a specific location in an array is handled by the hash operation. A hash operation will accept the key as input and return an integer that is used as an index into the hash table.

How does this work? The simplest case occurs when the key is an integer. Then the hash function could simply return an integer. For instance, given the key 3, the hash function would return the index value 3 to place the record in the hash table position 3. The key 1 would be used to place the record in hash table position 1.

Index	0	1	2	3	4	5	6
Key		1		3			

But what about a key value of 8? The array used to implement the hash table does not have a valid position 8, so some set of operations must be performed on the key in order to map it to an index value that is valid for the array. A simple solution to this problem is to perform a modulus operation with the table size on the key value. Using the example of 8 for the table of size 7 above, the hash function would calculate 8 modulus 7 to produce an index value of 1.

Unfortunately, it is easy for the hash calculation to generate the same index value for more than one key. This is called a **collision**. Using a key of 10 in the example above, the hash calculation would produce 3—calculated as 10 modulus 7 (10%7 in C++). But position 3 already has a key associated with it—the key 3. There are a number of methods that can be used to resolve the collision. The one we use is called **chaining**. When using chaining, all the keys that generate a particular index are connected to that array position in a chain. One way to implement chaining is by associating a list with each table entry. Using this approach, position 0 in the hash table would have a list of all data items for which the hash operation produces an index of 0, position 1 would have a list of all data items associated with index 1, and so on through index 6. The key values 1, 3, 7, 8, 10, and 13 would produce the following chains associated with the indexes 0, 1, 3, and 6.

Index	0	1	2	3	4	5	6
Key	7	1		3			13
		8		10			

Generating an index for other key types is more complicated than generating an index for integers. For instance, if the key for a record is a string, the string could be mapped to an integer by adding up the ASCII values of each of the characters in the string. Given a last name of "smith", the function could calculate a value of 115 ('s') + 109 ('m') + 105 ('i') + 116 ('t') + 104 ('h') = 549. Real numbers can be mapped to integers by simply truncating the noninteger part.

Note that these are simple examples of hash operations intended as an introduction to hash tables. A more detailed explanation would go into great detail about how to take a key and move the bits around to produce a high-quality key that will ensure a fairly uniform distribution of data items throughout the table. See In-lab 3 for more detail.

Hash Table ADT

Data Items

The data items in a hash table are of generic type DT.

Structure

The hash table is an array of singly linked lists. The list into which a data item is placed is determined by the index calculated using the data item's hash operation. The placement within a particular list is determined by the chronological order in which the data items are inserted into the list—the earliest insertion takes place at the head of the list, the most recent at the end of the list. The ordering within a particular list is *not* a function of the data contained in the hash table data items. You interact with each list by using the standard list operations.

Operations

```
HashTbl ( int initTableSize ) throw ( bad_alloc )
```

Requirements:
None

Results:
Constructor. Creates the empty hash table.


```
~HashTbl ()
```

Requirements:
None

Results:
Destructor. Deallocates (frees) the memory used to store a list.

```
void insert ( const DT &newDataItem ) throw ( bad_alloc )
```

Requirements:
Hash table is not full.

Results:
Inserts `newDataItem` into the appropriate list. If a data item with the same key as `newDataItem` already exists in the list, then updates that data item's nonkey fields with `newDataItem`'s nonkey fields. Otherwise, it inserts it at the end of that list.

```
bool remove ( KF searchKey )
```

Requirements:
None

Results:
Searches the hash table for the data item with key `searchKey`. If the data item is found, then removes the data item and returns `true`. Otherwise, returns `false`.

```
bool retrieve ( KF searchKey, DT &dataItem )
```

Requirements:
None

Results:
Searches the hash table for the data item with key `searchKey`. If the data item is found, then copies the data item to `dataItem` and returns `true`. Otherwise, returns `false` with `dataItem` undefined.

```
void clear ()
```

Requirements:
None

Results:
Removes all data items in the hash table.

```
bool isEmpty () const
```

Requirements:
None

Results:
Returns `true` if a hash table is empty. Otherwise, returns `false`.

```
bool isFull () const
```

Requirements:
None

Results:
Returns `true` if a hash table is full. Otherwise, returns `false`.

```
void showStructure () const
```

Requirements:
None

Results:
Outputs the data items in a hash table. If the hash table is empty, outputs "Empty hash table". Note that this operation is intended for testing/debugging purposes only. It supports only list data items that are one of C++'s predefined data types (`int`, `char`, and so forth).

Laboratory 14: Cover Sheet

Name _____ Date _____

Section _____

Place a check mark in the *Assigned* column next to the exercises your instructor has assigned to you. Attach this cover sheet to the front of the packet of materials you submit following the laboratory.

Activities	Assigned: Check or list exercise numbers	Completed
Prelab Exercise		
Bridge Exercise		
In-lab Exercise 1		
In-lab Exercise 2		
In-lab Exercise 3		
Postlab Exercise 1		
Postlab Exercise 2		
Total		

Laboratory 14: Prelab Exercise

Name _____   Date _____

Section _____

You can implement a hash table in many ways. We have chosen to implement the hash table using chaining to resolve collisions. The singly linked list ADT provides a simple way of dealing with a chain of data items and is an opportunity to use one of your ADTs to implement another ADT. Your instructor may choose to let you use one of the STL (Standard Template Library) lists instead.

Step 1: Implement the operations in the Hash Table ADT using an array of lists to store the list data items. You need to store the number of hash table slots (`tableSize`) and the actual hash table itself (`dataTable`). Base your implementation on the following declarations from the file *hashtbl.h*. An implementation of the `showStructure` operation is given in the file *show14.cpp*. If you are using an STL list, modify the `showStructure` operation to work with that STL list.

```
template < class DT, class KF >
class HashTbl
{
    public:
        HashTbl ( int initTableSize );
        ~HashTbl ();

        void insert ( const DT &newDataItem) throw ( bad_alloc );
        bool remove ( KF searchKey );
        bool retrieve ( KF searchKey, DT &dataItem );
        void clear ();

        bool isEmpty () const;
        bool isFull () const;

        void showStructure () const;
    private:
        int tableSize;
        List<DT> *dataTable;
};
```

Step 2: Save your implementation of the Hash Table ADT in the file *hashtbl.cpp*. Be sure to document your code.

The following program was adapted from the Lab 4 (Ordered List ADT) prelab. It reads in account numbers and balances for a set of accounts. It then tries retrieving records using the account numbers as the keys. The primary change is that the `Account` struct needs to have a `hash()` function added to be usable with the hash table. We also removed the code outputting the accounts in ascending order based on their account numbers because an ordered traversal of the hash table is not something supported by this Hash Table ADT.

```cpp
// lab14-example1.cpp
#include <iostream>
#include <cmath>
#include "hashtbl.cpp"

using namespace std;

struct Account
{
    int acctNum;              // (Key) Account number
    float balance;            // Account balance

    int getKey () const { return acctNum; }
    int hash(int key) const { return abs( key ); }
};

void main()
{
    HashTbl<Account,int> accounts(11);    // List of accounts
    Account acct;                         // A single account
    int searchKey;                        // An account key

    // Read in information on a set of accounts.

    cout << endl << "Enter account information for 5 accounts: "
        << endl;

    for ( int i = 0; i < 5; i++ )
    {
        cin >> acct.acctNum >> acct.balance;
        accounts.insert(acct);
    }

    // Checks for accounts and prints records if found

    cout << endl;
    cout << "Enter account number: ";
    while ( cin >> searchKey )
    {
        if ( accounts.retrieve(searchKey,acct) )
            cout << acct.acctNum << " " << acct.balance << endl;
        else
            cout << "Account " << searchKey << " not found." << endl;
    }
};
```

Laboratory 14: Bridge Exercise

Name _____ Date _____

Section _____

Check with your instructor whether you are to complete this exercise prior to your lab period or during lab.

The test program in the file *test14.cpp* allows you to interactively test your implementation of the Hash Table ADT using the following commands.

Command	Action
+key	Insert (or update) data item with key value key.
−key	Remove the data item with the key value key.
?key	Retrieve the item with the specified key and output it.
E	Report whether the list is empty.
F	Report whether the list is full.
C	Clear the list.
Q	Quit the test program.

Step 1: Prepare a test plan for your implementation of the Hash Table ADT. Your test plan should cover the application of each operation. A test plan form follows.

Step 2: Execute your test plan. If you discover mistakes in your implementation, correct them and execute your test plan again.

Test Plan for the Operations in the Hash Table ADT

Test Case	Commands	Expected Result	Checked

Laboratory 14: In-lab Exercise 1

Name _____   Date _____

Section _____

One possible use for a hash table is to store computer user login usernames and passwords. Your program should load username/password sets from the file *password.dat* and insert them into the hash table until the end of file is reached on *password.dat*. There is one username/password set per line, as shown in the following example.

```
jack        broken.crown
jill        tumblin'down
mary        contrary
bopeep      sheep!lost
```

Your program will then present a login prompt, read one username, present a password prompt, read the password, and then print either "Authentication successful" or "Authentication failure", as shown in the following examples.

Login: `jack`

Password: `broken.crown`

Authentication successful

Login: `jill`

Password: `tumblingdown`

Authentication failure

This authentication loop is to be repeated until the end of input data (EOF) is reached on the console input stream (`cin`).

Step 1: Prepare a test plan that specifies how you will validate that your program works correctly.

Step 2: Create a program that will read in the usernames and passwords from *password.dat* and then allow the user to try authenticating usernames and passwords as shown so long as the user enters more data. Store your program in the file *login.cpp*.

Create an appropriate `struct` to hold the username/password sets in the hash table.

Step 3: Run your program and test according to your test plan. If you discover mistakes, correct them and execute your test plan again.

Test Plan for the Login Authentication Program

Test Case	Expected Result	Checked

Laboratory 14: In-lab Exercise 2

Name _____   Date _____

Section _____

A hash table insertion or retrieval with no collisions is an O(1) operation. Collisions reduce the O(1) behavior to something less desirable. There are two ways to reduce collisions:

- Increase the size of the table. As the table size increases, the statistical probability of collisions for unique keys decreases. The problem with arbitrarily increasing the table size is that the amount of physical memory is finite and to declare a wildly large table in the hope of reducing collisions wastes memory.
- Enhance the quality of the hash() function so that it produces fewer collisions. Ideally, unique keys have unique indexes into the hash table and no collisions. This is called a **perfect hash**. The problem with generating perfect hash tables is that the hash function must be carefully crafted to avoid collisions.

A **minimal perfect hash** is a hash table with the following two properties:

- The minimal property—the memory allocated to store the keywords is exactly large enough to hold the needed number of keys and no more. For *n* keys, there are exactly *n* table entries.
- The perfect property—locating a table entry requires at most one key comparison. There are no collisions. Consequently, no collision resolution is required.

Software developers like minimal perfect hash tables for specific sets of strings because of the performance boost. For instance, it is very helpful if a C++ compiler can perform an O(1) lookup on a string to determine whether it is a C++ reserved word.

Step 1: Develop a hash() function implementation that will produce a minimal perfect hash for the following seven C++ reserved words.

- double
- else
- if
- return
- switch
- void
- while

Use the following struct to hold the strings.

```
struct Identifier
{
    string ident;
    string getKey() const
            { return ident; }
    int hash( string key ) const
            { return . . . }
};
```

Step 2: Prepare a test plan that specifies how you will verify that your `hash()` function works correctly to generate a minimal perfect hash table.

Step 3: Implement a test program using the above `struct` to demonstrate that you have indeed developed a minimal perfect hash for the given seven C++ identifiers. Save your program in the file *perfect.cpp*. Use the provided `showStructure()` function to display the hash table after all the data has been entered.

Step 4: Execute your test program and consider the results according to your test plan. If you discover mistakes in your implementation of the `hash()` function, correct them and execute your test plan again.

Test Plan for the `hash()` function

Hash Formula	Expected Result	Checked

Laboratory 14: In-lab Exercise 3

Name _____ Date _____

Section _____

Performance of hash tables depends on how uniformly the keys are distributed among the table entries. In the ideal situation—a minimal perfect hash (see In-Lab Exercise 2)—there is exactly one data item per hash table entry. Unfortunately, minimal perfect hashes become progressively more difficult to generate as the number of data items increases. In the worst possible key distribution scenario, all the data items would be chained off one hash table entry and all the other table entries would be empty. This is essentially a list, and the performance benefits of the hash table are lost. Rather than try to develop a perfect hash, developers usually build a hash function that will attempt to distribute the keys uniformly across all the table entries. Each table entry will have the same—or almost the same—number of keys associated with it.

Suppose that you have developed a hash function that you believe does a satisfactory job of distributing keys over the table. A good question to ask is "How uniform a distribution is the hash function achieving?" The formal mathematical answers are beyond the scope of this lab manual. However, one simple way of calculating this is to calculate the **standard deviation** of the number of data items associated with each table entry. The standard deviation number does not claim to answer whether or not a particular hash operation is good or bad, but it can be used as a rough comparison among hash functions used with the same table size and set of keys. The smaller the number obtained, the closer the hash function comes to providing a uniform distribution.

The formula to calculate the standard deviation, s, is

$$ s = \sqrt{\frac{\sum (x - \overline{x})^2}{n - 1}} $$

where x represents the number of data items chained off the current table location, $\overline{x}$ represents the average number of data items chained off each table location, and n represents the number of array entries in the table.

Standard deviation is calculated as follows:

1. Calculate and save the average—or mean—number of data items per table entry.
2. For each table entry, calculate and save (*number of items* − *mean number of* items)^2.
3. Calculate the sum of all the values calculated in step 2.
4. Divide the result from step 3 by $n - 1$, where n is the number of hash table entries.
5. Calculate the square root of the result obtained in step 4. This is the standard deviation.

Implement the following new Hash Table ADT operation—stdDeviation—that will calculate the standard deviation for key distribution in the hash table.

```
double stdDeviation ( )
```

Requirements:
None

Results:
Computes the standard deviation for key distribution in the hash table and returns the result.

Step 1: Implement this operation and add it to the file *hashtbl.cpp*. A prototype for this operation is included in the declaration of the Hash Table class in the file *hashtbl.h*.

Step 2: The program in the file *tst14std.cpp* will read data into a hash table and test your stdDeviation operation. It has three predefined hash function algorithms defined. All but the first algorithm are initially commented out. Please take a moment to study the three hash algorithms. Compile the program, run it, and record the results for Hash Algorithm 1 in the data table that follows in the lab book.

Step 3: Comment out Hash Algorithm #1 and uncomment Hash Algorithm #2. Repeat the directions in Step 2, filling in the data table entries for Hash Algorithm #2. Then do the same for Hash Algorithm #3.

Step 4: Invent two hash algorithms and enter them under Hash Algorithm #4 and Hash Algorithm #5. Repeat the compile-run-record cycle for both of them.

Step 5: Which of the hash algorithms that you tested produced the best result? What was the best hash algorithm produced by someone in your class? Why did the better algorithms produce superior results? Discuss the results with your lab instructor.

Data Table for the stdDeviation Operation

Hash algorithm used	Expected relative distribution quality (good/fair/poor)	Standard deviation	Measured relative distribution quality (good/fair/poor)
Hash Algorithm #1 `return 0;`			

Hash Algorithm #2
`return int(str[0])*10 +`
`       str.length();`			

Hash Algorithm #3
`double val = 0;`
`for (int i=0;`
`    i<str.length();`
`    i++)`
`{ val += (val*1.1)+str[i];}`
 	
`return int(val);`			

Hash Algorithm #4			
Hash Algorithm #5			

Laboratory 14: Postlab Exercise 1

Name _____   Date _____

Section _____

Part A

Given a hash table of size T, containing N data items, develop worst-case, order-of-magnitude estimates of the execution time of the following Hash Table ADT operations, assuming they are implemented using singly linked lists for the chained data items and a reasonably uniform distribution of data item keys. Briefly explain your reasoning behind each estimate.

insert   O(   )

Explanation:

retrieve   O(   )

Explanation:

Part B

What if the chaining is implemented using a binary search tree instead of a singly linked list? Using the same assumptions as above, develop worst-case, order-of-magnitude estimates of the execution time of the following Hash Table ADT operations. Briefly explain your reasoning behind each estimate.

insert   O(   )

Explanation:

retrieve   O(   )

Explanation:

Laboratory 14: Postlab Exercise 2

Name _____ Date _____

Section _____

Part A

For some large number of data items (e.g., $N = 1,000,000$), would you rather use a binary search tree or a hash table for performing data retrieval? Explain your reasoning.

Part B

Assuming the same number of data items given above, would the binary search tree or the hash table be most memory efficient? Explain your assumptions and your reasoning.

Part C

If you needed to select either the binary search tree or the hash table as the best general-purpose data structure, which would you choose? Under what circumstances would you choose the other data structure as preferable? Explain your reasoning.

String ADT

In this laboratory you will:

■ Examine the flaws in the standard C and early C++ string representation

■ Implement a more robust string data type

■ Use the C++ operators `new` and `delete` to dynamically allocate and deallocate memory

■ Create a program that performs lexical analysis using your new string data type

■ Analyze the limitations of the default copy constructor and develop an improved copy constructor

Objectives

Overview

When computers were first introduced, they were popularly characterized as giant calculating machines. As you saw in your introductory programming course, this characterization ignores the fact that computers are equally adept at manipulating other forms of information, including alphanumeric characters.

C++ supports the manipulation of character data through the predefined data type char and the associated operations for the input, output, assignment, and comparison of characters. Most applications of character data require character sequences—or **strings**—rather than individual characters. A string can be represented in C++ using a one-dimensional array of characters. By convention, a string begins in array data item zero and is terminated by the null character ('\0'). (That is how C and original C++ represented strings. Although C++ now has a standard string class, many current programming APIs—Application Programming Interfaces—require a knowledge of the C string representation.)

Representing a string as an array of characters terminated by a null suffers from several defects, including the following:

- The subscript operator ([]) does not check that the subscript lies within the boundaries of the string—or even within the boundaries of the array holding the string, for that matter.
- Strings are compared using functions that have far different calling conventions than the familiar relational operators (==, <, >, and so forth).
- The assignment operator (=) simply copies a pointer, not the character data it points to. The code fragment below, for example, makes str2 point to the array already pointed to by str1. It does not create a new array containing the string "data".

```
char *str1 = "data",
     *str2;
str2 = str1;
```

Either the length of a string must be declared at compile-time or a program must explicitly allocate and deallocate the memory used to store a string. Declaring the length of a string at compile-time is often impossible, or at least inefficient. Allocating and deallocating the memory used by a string **dynamically** (that is, at run-time) allows the string length to be set (or changed) as a program executes. Unfortunately, it is very easy for a programmer to forget to include code to deallocate memory once a string is no longer needed. Memory lost in this way—called a **memory leak**—accumulates over time, gradually crippling or even crashing a program. This will eventually require the program or computer system to be restarted.

In this laboratory you will develop a String ADT that addresses these problems. The following String ADT specification includes a diverse set of operations for manipulating strings.

String ADT

Data Items

A set of characters, excluding the null character.

Structure

The characters in a string are in sequential (or linear) order—that is, the characters follow one after the other from the beginning of a string to its end.

Operations

```
String ( int numChars = 0 ) throw ( bad_alloc )
```

Requirements:
None

Results:
Default constructor. Creates an empty string. Allocates enough memory for a string containing numChars characters plus any delimiter that may be required by the implementation of the String ADT.

```
String ( const char *charSeq ) throw ( bad_alloc )
```

Requirements:
None

Results:
Conversion constructor. Creates a string containing the character sequence in the array pointed to by charSeq. Assumes that charSeq is a valid C-string terminated by the null character. Allocates enough memory for the characters in the string plus any delimiter that may be required by the implementation of the String ADT.

```
~String ()
```

Requirements:
None

Results:
Destructor. Deallocates (frees) the memory used to store a string.

```
int getLength () const
```

Requirements:
None

Results:
Returns the number of characters in a string (excluding the delimiter).

```
char operator [] ( int n ) const
```

Requirements:
None

Results:
Returns the *n*th character in a string—where the characters are numbered beginning with zero. If the string does not have an *n*th character, then returns the null character.

```
void operator = ( const String &rightString ) throw ( bad_alloc )
```

Requirements:
None

Results:
Assigns (copies) the contents of rightString to a string.

```
void clear ()
```

Requirements:
None

Results:
Clears a string, thereby making it an empty string.

```
void showStructure () const
```

Requirements:
None

Results:
Outputs the characters in a string, as well as the delimiter. Note that this operation is intended for testing/debugging purposes only.

Laboratory A: Cover Sheet

Name _____ Date _____

Section _____

Place a check mark in the *Assigned* column next to the exercises your instructor has assigned to you. Attach this cover sheet to the front of the packet of materials you submit following the laboratory.

Activities	Assigned: Check or list exercise numbers	Completed
Prelab Exercise		
Bridge Exercise		
In-lab Exercise 1		
In-lab Exercise 2		
In-lab Exercise 3		
Postlab Exercise 1		
Postlab Exercise 2		
Total		

Laboratory A: Prelab Exercise

Name _____   Date _____

Section _____

The first decision you must make when implementing the String ADT is how to store the characters in a string. In the Overview, you saw that original C++ represented a string as a null-terminated sequence of characters in a one-dimensional buffer. Adopting this representation scheme allows you to reuse existing C++ functions in your implementation of the String ADT. This code reuse, in turn, greatly simplifies the implementation process.

Your String ADT will be more flexible if you dynamically allocate the memory used by the string buffer. The initial memory allocation for a buffer is done by a constructor. One of the constructors is invoked whenever a string declaration is encountered during the execution of a program. Which one is invoked depends on whether the declaration has as its argument an integer or a string literal. Once called, the constructor allocates a string buffer using C++'s new function. The following constructor, for example, allocates a string buffer of bufferSize characters and assigns the address of the string buffer to the pointer buffer, where buffer is of type char*.

```
String:: String ( int numChars )
{
    ...
    buffer = new char [bufferSize];
}
```

Whenever you allocate memory, you must ensure that it is deallocated when it is no longer needed. The class destructor is used to deallocate a string buffer. This function is invoked whenever a string variable goes out of scope—that is, whenever the function containing the corresponding variable declaration terminates. The fact that the call to the destructor is made automatically eliminates the possibility of you forgetting to deallocate the buffer. The following destructor frees the memory used by the string buffer allocated above.

```
String:: ~String ()
{
    ...
    delete [] buffer;
}
```

Constructors and destructors are not the only operations that allocate and deallocate memory. The assignment operation also may need to perform memory allocation/deallocation in order to extend the length of a string buffer to accommodate additional characters.

Strings can be of various lengths, and the length of a given string can change as a result of an assignment. Your string representation should account for these variations in length by storing the length of a string (bufferSize) along with a pointer to the buffer containing the characters in the string (buffer). The resulting string representation is described by the following declarations:

```
int bufferSize;    // Size of the string buffer
char *buffer;      // String buffer containing a null-terminated
                   // sequence of characters
```

Step 1: Implement the operations in the String ADT using this string representation scheme. Base your implementation on the following class declaration from the file *stradt.h*.

```cpp
class String
{
  public:

    // Constructors
    String ( int numChars = 0 )
        throw ( bad_alloc );                    // Create an empty string
    String ( const char *charSeq )
        throw ( bad_alloc );                    // Initialize using char*

    // Destructor
    ~String ();

    // String operations
    int getLength () const;                     // # characters
    char operator [] ( int n ) const;           // Subscript
    void operator = ( const String &rightString )   // Assignment
        throw ( bad_alloc );
    void clear ();                              // Clear string

    // Output the string structure - used in testing/debugging
    void showStructure () const;

  private:

    // Data members
    int bufferSize;          // Size of the string buffer
    char *buffer;            // String buffer containing a null-terminated
};                           // sequence of characters
```

Step 2: Save your implementation of the String ADT in the file *stradt.cpp*. Be sure to document your code.

Laboratory A: Bridge Exercise

Name _____ Date _____

Section _____

Check with your instructor whether you are to complete this exercise prior to your lab period or during lab.

Test your implementation of the String ADT using the program in the file *testa.cpp*. This program supports the following tests.

Test	Action
1	Tests the constructors.
2	Tests the length operation.
3	Tests the subscript operation.
4	Tests the assignment and clear operations.

Step 1: Compile your implementation of the String ADT in the file *stradt.cpp*.

Step 2: Compile the test program in the file *testa.cpp*.

Step 3: Link the object files produced by Steps 1 and 2.

Step 4: Complete the test plan for Test 1 by filling in the expected result for each string.

Step 5: Execute the test plan. If you discover mistakes in your implementation of the String ADT, correct them and execute the test plan again.

Test Plan for Test 1 (Constructors)

Test Case	String	Expected Result	Checked
Simple string	alpha	alpha	
Longer string	epsilon		
Single-character string	a		
Empty string	*empty*		

Step 6: Complete the test plan for Test 2 by filling in the length of each string.

Step 7: Execute the test plan. If you discover mistakes in your implementation of the String ADT, correct them and execute the test plan again.

Test Plan for Test 2 (length Operation)

Test Case	String	Expected Length	Checked
Simple string	alpha	5	
Longer string	epsilon		
Single-character string	a		
Empty string	*empty*		

Step 8: Complete the test plan for Test 3 by filling in the character returned by subscript operation for each value of *n* and the string "alpha".

Step 9: Execute the test plan. If you discover mistakes in your implementation of the String ADT, correct them and execute the test plan again.

Test Plan for Test 3 (subscript Operation)

Test case	n	Expected character	Checked
Middle character	2	p	
First character	0		
Last character	4		
Out of range	10		

Step 10: Complete the test plan for Test 4 by filling in the expected result for each assignment statement.

Step 11: Execute the test plan. If you discover mistakes in your implementation of the String ADT, correct them and execute the test plan again.

Test Plan for Test 4 (assignment and clear Operations)

Test Case	Assignment Statement	Expected Result	Checked
Simple assignment	assignStr = alpha;	alpha	
Single-character string	assignStr = a;		
Empty string	assignStr = *empty*;		
Source string longer than destination buffer	assignStr = epsilon;		
Assign to self	assignStr = assignStr;		
Check assignment by clearing destination	assignStr = alpha; assignStr.clear();		

Laboratory A: In-lab Exercise 1

Name _____ Date _____

Section _____

A compiler begins the compilation process by dividing a program into a set of delimited strings called **tokens**. This task is referred to as **lexical analysis**. For instance, given the C++ statement,

```
if ( j <= 10 ) cout << endl ;
```

lexical analysis by a C++ compiler produces the following ten tokens:

"if" "(" "j" "<=" "10" ")" "cout" "<<" "endl" ";"

Before you can perform lexical analysis, you need operations that support the input and output of delimited strings. A pair of String ADT input/output operations are described below.

```
friend istream & operator >> ( istream &input,
                               String &inputString )
```

Requirements:
The specified input stream must not be in an error state.

Returns:
Extracts (inputs) a string from the specified input stream, returns it in `inputString`, and returns the resulting state of the input stream. Begins the input process by reading whitespace (blanks, newlines, and tabs) until a non-whitespace character is encountered. This character is returned as the first character in the string. Continues reading the string character by character until another whitespace character is encountered.

```
friend ostream & operator << ( ostream &output,
                               const String &outputString )
```

Requirements:
The specified output stream must not be in an error state.

Returns:
Inserts (outputs) `outputString` in the specified output stream and returns the resulting state of the output stream.

Note that these operations are *not* part of the String class. However, they do need to have access to the data members of this class. Thus, they are named as **friends** of the String class.

Step 1: The file *strio.cpp* contains implementations of these string input/output operations. Add these operations to your implementation of the String ADT in the file *stradt.cpp*. Prototypes for these operations are included in the declaration of String class in the file *stradt.h*.

Step 2: Create a program (stored in the file *lexical.cpp*) that uses the operations in the String ADT to perform lexical analysis on a text file containing a C++ program. Your program should read the tokens in this file and output each token to the screen using the following format:

```
1 : [1stToken]
2 : [2ndToken]
...
```

This format requires that your program maintain a running count of the number of tokens that have been read from the text file. Assume that the tokens in the text file are delimited by whitespace—an assumption that is not true for C++ programs in general.

Step 3: Test your lexical analysis program using the C++ program in the file *progsamp.dat*. The contents of this file are shown below.

```
void main ( )
{
    int j ,
    total = 0 ;
    for ( j = 1 ; j <= 20 ; j ++ )
        total += j ;
}
```

Test Plan for the Lexical Analysis Program

Test Case	Expected Result	Checked
Program in the file *progsamp.dat*		

Laboratory A: In-lab Exercise 2

Name _____ Date _____

Section _____

Whenever an argument is passed to a function using call by value, the compiler makes a copy of the argument. The function then manipulates this copy rather than the original argument. Once the function terminates, the copy is deleted.

How does the compiler know how to construct a copy of a particular argument? For C++'s predefined types, this task is straightforward. The compiler simply makes a **bitwise** (bit by bit) copy of the argument. Unfortunately, this approach does not work well with instances of the String class. Consider what happens when the call

```
dummy(testStr);
```

is made to the following function:

```
void dummy ( String valueStr );
```

A bitwise copy of string `testStr` to string `valueStr` copies pointer `testStr.buffer` to pointer `valueStr.buffer`. The string buffer pointed to by `testStr.buffer` is not copied and there are now two pointers to the same string buffer. As a result, changes to `valueStr` also change `testStr`, clearly violating the constraints of call by value. In addition, when the function terminates, the String class destructor is called to delete the copy (`valueStr`). As it deletes `valueStr`'s string buffer, the destructor also is deleting `testStr`'s string buffer.

Fortunately, C++ provides us with a method for addressing this problem. We can specify exactly how a copy is to be created by including a **copy constructor** in our String class. The compiler then uses our copy constructor in place of its default (bitwise) copy constructor. A copy constructor for the String class is described below.

```
String ( const String &valueString ) throw ( bad_alloc )
```

Requirements:
None

Results:
Copy constructor. Creates a copy of `valueString`. This constructor is invoked automatically whenever a string is passed to a function using call by value, a function returns a string, or a string is initialized using another string.

Step 1: Implement this operation and add it to the file *stradt.cpp*. A prototype for this operation is included in the declaration of the String class in the file *stradt.h*.

Step 2: Activate Test 5 in the test program *testa.cpp* by removing the comment delimiter (and the character "5") from the lines that begin with "//5".

Step 3: Complete the test plan for Test 5 by filling in the expected result for each string.

Step 4: Execute the test plan. If you discover mistakes in your implementation of the copy constructor, correct them and execute the test plan again.

Test Plan for Test 5 (Copy Constructor)

Test Case	String Argument	Expected Result	Checked
Simple string	alpha	alpha	
Single-character	a		

Laboratory A: In-lab Exercise 3

Name _____ Date _____

Section _____

Most applications that use strings will at some point sort the string data into alphabetical order, either to make their output easier to read or to improve program performance. In order to sort strings, you first must develop relational operations that compare strings with one another.

```
bool operator == ( const String &leftString,
                   const String &rightString )
```

Requirements:
None

Results:
Returns true if leftString is the same as rightString. Otherwise, returns false.

```
bool operator < ( const String &leftString,
                  const String &rightString )
```

Requirements:
None

Results:
Returns true if leftString is less than rightString. Otherwise, returns false.

```
bool operator > ( const String &leftString,
                  const String &rightString )
```

Requirements:
None

Results:
Returns true if leftString is greater than rightString. Otherwise, returns false.

All these operations require moving through a pair of strings in parallel from beginning to end, comparing characters until a difference (if any) is found between the strings. They vary in how they interpret this difference.

The standard C++ C-string library includes a function strcmp() that can be used to compare strings character by character. Alternatively, you can develop your own private member function to perform this task.

Step 1: Implement the relational operations described above using the C++ strcmp() function (or your own private member function) as a foundation. Add your implementation of these operations to the file *stradt.cpp*. Prototypes for these operations are included in the declaration of the String class in the file *stradt.h*.

Step 2: Activate Test 6 in the test program *testa.cpp* by removing the comment delimiter (and the character '6') from the lines that begin with "//6".

Step 3: Complete the test plan for Test 6 by filling in the expected result for each pair of strings.

Step 4: Execute the test plan. If you discover mistakes in your implementation of the relational operations, correct them and execute the test plan again.

Test Plan for Test 6 (Relational Operations)

Test case	Pair of strings	Expected result	Checked
Second string greater	alpha epsilon		
First string greater	epsilon alpha		
Identical strings	alpha alpha		
First string embedded in second	alp alpha		
Second string embedded in first	alpha alpha		
First string is a single character	a alpha		
Second string is a single character	alpha a		
First string is empty	*empty* alpha		
Second string is empty	alpha *empty*		
Both strings are empty	*empty empty*		

Laboratory A: Postlab Exercise 1

Name _____ Date _____

Section _____

In In-lab Exercise 2, you saw that a class's default copy constructor can cause problems if the class contains a pointer. Comment out the declaration of the copy constructor in the file *stradt.h* and your implementation of this constructor in the file *stradt.cpp* (assuming you created one in In-lab Exercise 2). This forces you to use the default copy constructor.

Using the default copy constructor, execute Steps 2, 3, and 4 of In-lab Exercise 2 and explain the results below.

Laboratory A: Postlab Exercise 2

Name _____   Date _____

Section _____

Part A

Design another operation for the String ADT and give its specification below. You need not implement the operation, simply describe it.

Requirements:

Results:

Part B

Describe an application in which you might you use your new operation.

Heap ADT

In this laboratory you will:

- Create an implementation of the Heap ADT using an array representation of a tree

- Use inheritance to derive a priority queue class from your heap class and develop a simulation of an operating system's task scheduler using a priority queue

- Create a heap sort function based on the heap construction techniques used in your implementation of the Heap ADT

- Analyze where data items with various priorities are located in a heap

Overview

Linked structures are not the only way in which you can represent trees. If you take the binary tree shown below and copy its contents into an array in level order, you produce the following array.

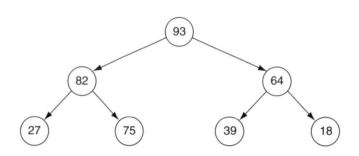

Index	Entry
0	93
1	82
2	64
3	27
4	75
5	39
6	18

Examining the relationship between positions in the tree and entries in the array, you see that if a data item is stored in entry N in the array, then the data item's left child is stored in entry $2N + 1$, its right child is stored in entry $2N + 2$, and its parent is stored in entry $(N - 1)$ mod 2. These mappings make it easy to move through the tree stepping from parent to child (or vice versa).

You could use these mappings to support an array-based implementation of the Binary Search Tree ADT. However, the result would be a tree representation in which large areas of the array are left unused (as indicated by the "−" character in the following array).

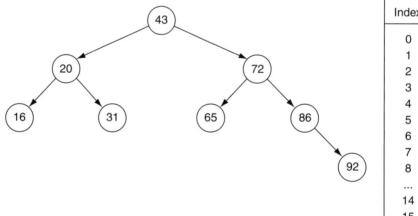

Index	Entry
0	43
1	20
2	72
3	16
4	31
5	65
6	86
7	−
8	−
...	...
14	−
15	92

In this laboratory, you focus on a different type of tree called a heap. A **heap** is a binary tree that meets the following conditions.

- The tree is **complete**. That is, every level in the tree is full, except possibly the bottom level. If the bottom level is not full, then all the missing data items occur on the right.
- Each data item in the tree has a corresponding priority value. For each data item E, all of E's descendants have priorities that are less than or equal to E's priority. Note that priorities are *not* unique.

The tree shown on the first page of this laboratory is a heap, as is the tree shown below.

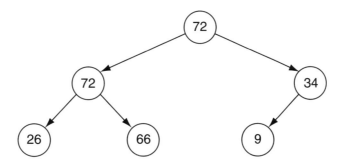

The fact that the tree is complete means that a heap can be stored in level order in an array without introducing gaps (unused areas) in the middle. The result is a compact representation in which you can easily move up and down the branches.

Clearly, the relationship between the priorities of the various data items in a heap is not strong enough to support an efficient search process. Because the relationship is simple, however, you can quickly restructure a heap after removing the highest priority (root) data item or after inserting a new data item. As a result, you can rapidly process the data items in a heap in descending order based on priority. This property combined with the compact array representation makes a heap an ideal representation for a priority queue (In-lab Exercise 1) and forms the basis for an efficient sorting algorithm called heap sort (In-lab Exercise 2).

Heap ADT

Data Items

The data items in a heap are of generic type DT. Each data item has a priority that is used to determine the relative position of the data item within the heap. Data items usually include additional data. Note that priorities are *not* unique—it is quite likely that several data items have the same priority. Objects of type DT must provide a function called pty() that returns a data item's priority. You must be able to compare priorities using the six basic relational operators.

Structure

The data items form a complete binary tree. For each data item E in the tree, all of E's descendants have priorities that are less than or equal to E's priority.

Operations

```
Heap ( int maxNumber = defMaxHeapSize )
```

Requirements:
None

Results:
Constructor. Creates an empty heap. Allocates enough memory for a heap containing maxNumber data items.

```
~Heap ()
```

Requirements:
None

Results:
Destructor. Deallocates (frees) the memory used to store a heap.

```
void insert ( const DT &newDataItem ) throw ( logic_error )
```

Requirements:
Heap is not full.

Results:
Inserts `newDataItem` into a heap. Inserts this data item as the bottom rightmost data item in the heap and moves it upward until the properties that define a heap are restored.

```
DT removeMax () throw ( logic_error )
```

Requirements:
Heap is not empty.

Results:
Removes the data item with the highest priority (the root) from a heap and returns it. Replaces the root data item with the bottom rightmost data item and moves this data item downward until the properties that define a heap are restored.

```
void clear ()
```

Requirements:
None

Results:
Removes all the data items in a heap.

```
bool isEmpty () const
```

Requirements:
None

Results:
Returns `true` if a heap is empty. Otherwise, returns `false`.

```
bool isFull () const
```

Requirements:
None

Results:
Returns `true` if a heap is full. Otherwise, returns `false`.

```
void showStructure () const
```

Requirements:
None

Results:
Outputs the priorities of the data items in a heap in both array and tree form. The tree is output with its branches oriented from left (root) to right (leaves)—that is, the tree is output rotated counterclockwise 90 degrees from its conventional orientation. If the heap is empty, outputs "Empty heap". Note that this operation is intended for testing/debugging purposes only.

Laboratory B: Cover Sheet

Name _____ Date _____

Section _____

Place a check mark in the *Assigned* column next to the exercises your instructor has assigned to you. Attach this cover sheet to the front of the packet of materials you submit following the laboratory.

Activities	Assigned: Check or list exercise numbers	Completed
Prelab Exercise		
Bridge Exercise		
In-lab Exercise 1		
In-lab Exercise 2		
In-lab Exercise 3		
Postlab Exercise 1		
Postlab Exercise 2		
Total		

Laboratory B: Prelab Exercise

Name _____ Date _____

Section _____

Step 1: Implement the operations in the Heap ADT using an array representation of a heap. Heaps can be different sizes; therefore, you need to store the maximum number of data items the heap can hold (maxSize) and the actual number of data items in the heap (size), along with the heap data items themselves (dataItems). Base your implementation on the following declarations from the file *heap.h*. An implementation of the showStructure operation is given in the file *showb.cpp*.

```cpp
const int defMaxHeapSize = 10;     // Default maximum heap size

template < class DT >
class Heap
{
  public:

    // Constructor
    Heap ( int maxNumber = defMaxHeapSize ) throw ( bad_alloc );

    // Destructor
    ~Heap ();

    // Heap manipulation operations
    void insert ( const DT &newDataItem )      // Insert data item
        throw ( logic_error );
    DT removeMax () throw ( logic_error );      // Remove max pty data item
    void clear ();                             // Clear heap

    // Heap status operations
    int isEmpty () const;                      // Heap is empty
    int isFull () const;                       // Heap is full

    // Output the heap structure - used in testing/debugging
    void showStructure () const;

  private:

    // Recursive partner of the showStructure() function
    void showSubtree ( int index, int level ) const;

    // Data members
    int maxSize,                  // Maximum number of data items in the heap
        size;                     // Actual number of data items in the heap
    DT *dataItems;                // Array containing the heap data items
};
```

Step 2: Save your implementation of the Heap ADT in the file *heap.cpp*. Be sure to document your code.

Laboratory B: Bridge Exercise

Name _____ Date _____

Section _____

Check with your instructor whether you are to complete this exercise prior to your lab period or during lab.

The test program in the file *testb.cpp* allows you to interactively test your implementation of the Heap ADT using the following commands.

Command	Action
+pty	Insert a data item with the specified priority.
–	Remove the data item with the highest priority from the heap and output it.
E	Report whether the heap is empty.
F	Report whether the heap is full.
C	Clear the heap.
Q	Quit the test program.

Step 1: Prepare a test plan for your implementation of the Heap ADT. Your test plan should cover heaps of various sizes, including empty, full, and single data item heaps. A test plan form follows.

Step 2: Execute your test plan. If you discover mistakes in your implementation, correct them and execute your test plan again.

Test Plan for the Operations in the Heap ADT

Test Case	Commands	Expected Result	Checked

Laboratory B: In-lab Exercise 1

Name _____ Date _____

Section _____

A **priority queue** is a linear data structure in which the data items are maintained in descending order based on priority. You can only access the data item at the front of the queue—that is, the data item with the highest priority—and examining this data item entails removing (dequeuing) it from the queue.

Priority Queue ADT

Data Items

The data items in a priority queue are of generic type DT. Each data item has a priority that is used to determine the relative position of the data item within the queue. Data items usually include additional data. Objects of type DT must supply a function called `pty()` that returns a data item's priority. You must be able to compare priorities using the six basic relational operators.

Structure

The queue data items are stored in descending order based on priority.

Operations

```
Queue ( int maxNumber = defMaxQueueSize )
```

Requirements:
None

Results:
Constructor. Creates an empty priority queue. Allocates enough memory for a queue containing `maxNumber` data items.

```
~Queue ()
```

Requirements:
None

Results:
Destructor. Deallocates (frees) the memory used to store a priority queue.

```
void enqueue ( const DT &newDataItem ) throw ( logic_error )
```

Requirements:
Queue is not full.

Results:
Inserts `newDataItem` into a priority queue.

```
DT dequeue () throw ( logic_error )
```

Requirements:
Queue is not empty.

Results:
Removes the highest priority (front) data item from a priority queue and returns it.

```
void clear ()
```

Requirements:
None

Results:
Removes all the data items in a priority queue.

```
bool isEmpty () const
```

Requirements:
None

Results:
Returns `true` if a priority queue is empty. Otherwise, returns `false`.

```
bool isFull () const
```

Requirements:
None

Results:
Returns `true` if a priority queue is full. Otherwise, returns `false`.

You can easily and efficiently implement a priority queue as a heap by using the Heap ADT `insert` operation to enqueue data items and the `removeMax` operation to dequeue data items. The following declarations from the file *ptyqueue.h* derive a class called PtyQueue from the Heap class. If you are unfamiliar with the C++ inheritance mechanism, read the discussion in Laboratory 4.

```
const int defMaxQueueSize = 10;   // Default maximum queue size

template < class DT >
class PtyQueue : public Heap<DT>
{
  public:

    // Constructor
    PtyQueue ( int maxNumber = defMaxQueueSize );

    // Queue manipulation operations
    void enqueue ( const DT &newDataItem ) throw ( logic_error );
                                            // Enqueue data data item
    DT dequeue () throw ( logic_error );
                                            // Dequeue data data item
};
```

Implementations of the Priority Queue ADT constructor, enqueue, and dequeue operations are given in the file *ptyqueue.cpp*. These implementations are very short, reflecting the close relationship between the Heap ADT and the Priority Queue ADT. Note that you inherit the remaining operations in the Priority Queue ADT from the Heap class.

Operating systems commonly use priority queues to regulate access to system resources such as printers, memory, disks, software, and so forth. Each time a task requests access to a system resource, the task is placed on the priority queue associated with that resource. When the task is dequeued, it is granted access to the resource—to print, store data, and so on.

Suppose you wish to model the flow of tasks through a priority queue having the following properties:

- One task is dequeued every minute (assuming that there is at least one task waiting to be dequeued during that minute).
- From zero to two tasks are enqueued every minute, where there is a 50% chance that no tasks are enqueued, a 25% percent chance that one task is enqueued, and a 25% chance that two tasks are enqueued.
- Each task has a priority value of zero (low) or one (high), where there is an equal chance of a task having either of these values.

You can simulate the flow of tasks through the queue during a time period *n* minutes long using the following algorithm.

```
Initialize the queue to empty.
for ( minute = 0 ; minute < n ; ++minute )
{
    If the queue is not empty, then remove the task at the front of the queue.
    Compute a random integer k between 0 and 3.
    If k is 1, then add one task to the queue. If k is 2, then add two tasks.
        Otherwise (if k is 0 or 3), do not add any tasks to the queue. Compute the
        priority of each task by generating a random value of 0 or 1.
}
```

Step 1: Using the program shell given in the file *ossim.cs* as a basis, create a program that uses the Priority Queue ADT to implement the task scheduler described above. Your program should output the following information about each task as it is dequeued: the task's priority, when it was enqueued, and how long it waited in the queue.

Step 2: Use your program to simulate the flow of tasks through the priority queue and complete the following table.

Time (minutes)	Longest wait for any low-priority (0) task	Longest wait for any high-priority (1) task
10		
30		
60		

Step 3: Is your priority queue task scheduler unfair—that is, given two tasks T_1 and T_2 of the same priority, where task T_1 is enqueued at time N and task T_2 is enqueued at time $N + i$ ($i > 0$), is task T_2 ever dequeued before task T_1? If so, how can you eliminate this problem and make your task scheduler fair?

Laboratory B: In-lab Exercise 2

Name _____ Date _____

Section _____

After removing the root data item, the `removeMax` operation inserts a new data item at the root and moves this data item downward until a heap is produced. The following function performs a similar task, except that the heap it is building is rooted at array entry root and occupies only a portion of the array.

```
void moveDown ( DT dataItems [], int root, int size )
```

Input:
The left and right subtrees of the binary tree rooted at `root` are heaps. Parameter `size` is the number of elements in the tree.

Output:
Restores the binary tree rooted at `root` to a heap by moving `dataItems[root]` downward until the tree satisfies the heap property.

In this exercise, you implement an efficient sorting algorithm called **heap sort** using the `moveDown()` function. You first use this function to transform an array into a heap. You then remove data items one by one from the heap (from the highest priority data item to the lowest) until you produce a sorted array.

Let's begin by examining how you transform an unsorted array into a heap. Each leaf of any binary tree is a one-data item heap. You can build a heap containing three data items from a pair of sibling leaves by applying the `moveDown()` function to that pair's parent. The four single data item heaps (leaf nodes) in the following tree are transformed by the calls `moveDown(dataItems,1,7)` and `moveDown(dataItems,2,7)` into a pair of three data item heaps.

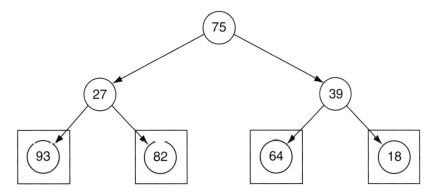

Index	Entry
0	75
1	27
2	39
3	93
4	82
5	64
6	18

By repeating this process, you build larger and larger heaps, until you transform the entire tree (array) into a heap.

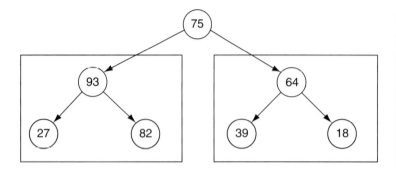

Index	Entry
0	75
1	93
2	64
3	27
4	82
5	39
6	18

```
// Build successively larger heaps within the array until the
// entire array is a heap.

for ( j = (size-1)/2 ; j >= 0 ; j-- )
      moveDown(dataItems,j,size);
```

Combining the pair of three-data item heaps shown above using the call `moveDown(dataItems,0,7)`, for instance, produces the following heap.

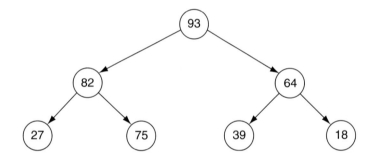

Index	Entry
0	93
1	82
2	64
3	27
4	75
5	39
6	18

Now that you have a heap, you remove data items of decreasing priority from the heap and gradually construct an array that is sorted in ascending order. The root of the heap contains the highest-priority data item. If you swap the root with the data item at the end of the array and use `moveDown()` to form a new heap, you end up with a heap containing six data items and a sorted array containing one data item. Performing this process a second time yields a heap containing five data items and a sorted array containing two data items.

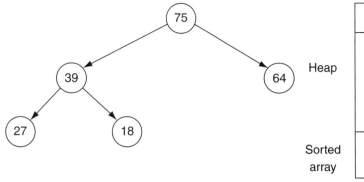

Index	Entry
0	75
1	39
2	64
3	27
4	18
5	82
6	93

Heap

Sorted array

You repeat this process until the heap is gone and a sorted array remains.

```
// Swap the root data item from each successively smaller heap with
// the last unsorted data item in the array. Restore the heap after
// each exchange.

for ( j = size-1 ; j > 0 ; j-- )
{
    temp = dataItems[j];
    dataItems[j] = dataItems[0];
    dataItems[0] = temp;
    moveDown(dataItems,0,j);
}
```

A shell containing a heapSort() function comprised of the two loops shown above is given in the file *heapsort.cs*.

Step 1: Using your implementation of the removeMax operation as a basis, create an implementation of the moveDown() function.

Step 2: Add your implementation of the movedown() function to the shell in the file *heapsort.cs* thereby completing code needed by the heapSort() function. Save the result in the file *heapsort.cpp*.

Step 3: Before testing the resulting heapSort() function using the test program in the file *testbhs.cpp*, prepare a test plan for the heapSort() function that covers arrays of different lengths containing a variety of priority values. Be sure to include arrays that have multiple data items with the same priority. A test plan form follows.

Step 4: Execute your test plan. If you discover mistakes in your implementation of the moveDown() function, correct them and execute your test plan again.

Test Plan for the heapSort Operation

Test Case	Array	Expected Result	Checked

Laboratory B: In-lab Exercise 3

Name _____   Date _____

Section _____

Examining the tree form of a heap rotated 90 degrees counterclockwise from its conventional orientation can be awkward. Because a heap is a complete tree, an unambiguous representation in tree form can be generated by outputting the heap level by level, with each level output on a separate line.

```
void writeLevels () const
```

Requirements:
None

Results:
Outputs the data items in a heap in level order, one level per line. Only outputs each data item's priority. If the heap is empty, then outputs "Empty heap".

The tree shown on the first page of this laboratory, for example, yields the following output.

```
93
82 64
27 75 39 18
```

Step 1: Implement this operation and add it to the file *heap.cpp*. A prototype for this operation is included in the declaration of the Heap class in the file *heap.h*.

Step 2: Activate the 'W' (write levels) command in the test program in the file *testb.cpp* by removing the comment delimiter (and the character 'W') from the lines that begin with "//W".

Step 3: Prepare a test plan for this operation that covers heaps of various sizes, including empty and single-data item heaps. A test plan form follows.

Step 4: Execute your test plan. If you discover mistakes in your implementation of the writeLevels operation, correct them and execute your test plan again.

Test Plan for the `writeLevels` Operation

Test Case	Commands	Expected Result	Checked

Laboratory B: Postlab Exercise 1

Name _____ Date _____

Section _____

You can use a heap—or a priority queue (In-lab Exercise 1)—to implement both a first-in, first-out (FIFO) queue and a stack. The trick is to use the order in which data items arrive as the basis for determining the data items' priority values.

Part A

How would you assign priority values to data items to produce a FIFO queue?

Part B

How would you assign priority values to data items to produce a stack?

Laboratory B: Postlab Exercise 2

Name _____ Date _____

Section _____

Part A

Given a heap containing 10 data items with distinct priorities, where in the heap can the data item with the next-to-highest priority be located? Give examples to illustrate your answer.

Part B

Given the same heap as in Part A, where in the heap can the data item with the lowest priority be located? Give examples to illustrate your answer.

Performance Evaluation

In this laboratory you will:

- Implement a Timer class that you can use to measure the length time between two events—when a function starts and when it finishes, for instance

- Compare the performance of a set of searching routines

- Compare the performance of a set of sorting routines

- Compare the performance of your array and linked list implementations of the Stack ADT

Overview

A routine's performance can be judged in many ways and on many levels. In other laboratories, you describe performance using order-of-magnitude estimates of a routine's execution time. You develop these estimates by analyzing how the routine performs its task, paying particular attention to how it uses iteration and recursion. You then express the routine's projected execution time as a function of the number of data items (N) that it manipulates as it performs its task. The results are estimates of the form O(N), O(LogN), and so on.

These order-of-magnitude estimates allow you to group routines based on their projected performance under different conditions (best case, worst case, and so forth). As important as these order-of-magnitude estimates are, they are by their very nature only estimates. They do not take into account factors specific to a particular environment, such as how a routine is implemented, the type of computer system on which it is being run, and the kind of data being processed. If you are to accurately determine how well or poorly a given routine will perform in a particular environment, you need to evaluate the routine in that environment.

In this laboratory, you measure the performance of a variety of routines. You begin by developing a set of tools that allow you to measure execution time. Then you use these tools to measure the execution times of the routines.

You can determine a routine's execution time in a number of ways. The timings performed in this laboratory will be generated using the approach summarized below.

Get the current system time (call this *startTime*).

Execute the routine.

Get the current system time (call this *stopTime*).

The routine's execution time = *startTime* − *stopTime*.

If the routine executes very rapidly, then the difference between `startTime` and `stopTime` may be too small for your computer system to measure. Should this be the case, you need to execute the routine several times and divide the length of the resulting time interval by the number of repetitions, as follows:

Get the current system time (call this *startTime*).

Execute the routine *m* times.

Get the current system time (call this *stopTime*).

The routine's execution time = (*startTime* − *stopTime*) / *m*.

To use this approach, you must have some method for getting and storing the "current system time". How the current system time is defined and how it is accessed varies from system to system. Two common methods are outlined below.

Method 1

Use a function call to get the amount of processor time that your program (or process) has used. Typically, the processor time is measured in clock ticks or fractions of a second. Store this information in a variable of the following type:

```
typedef long SystemTime;
```

You can use this method on most systems. You must use it on multiuser or multiprocess systems, where the routine you are timing is not the only program running.

Method 2

Use a function call to get the current time of day. Store this information in a variable of the following type:

```
struct SystemTime
{
    int hour,       // Hour    0-23
        minute,     // Minute 0-59
        second,     // Second 0-59
        fraction;   // Fraction of a second
};
```

The range of values for the fraction field depends on the resolution of the system clock. Common ranges are 0–99 (hundredths of a second) and 0–999 (thousandths of a second). This method is effective only on single-user/single-process systems where the routine you are timing is the only program running.

In addition to acquiring and storing a point in time, you also need a convenient mechanism for measuring time intervals. The Timer ADT described below uses the familiar stopwatch metaphor to describe the timing process.

Start the timer.

...

Stop the timer.

Read the elapsed time.

Timer ADT

Data Items

A pair of times that denote the beginning and end of a time interval.

Structure

None

Operations

```
void start ()
```

Requirements
None

Results
Marks the beginning of a time interval (starts the timer).

```
void stop ()
```

Requirements
The beginning of a time interval has been marked.

Results
Marks the end of a time interval (stops the timer).

```
double getElapsedTime ()
```

Requirements
The beginning and end of a time interval have been marked.

Results
Returns the length of the time interval in seconds.

Laboratory C: Cover Sheet

Name _____ Date _____

Section _____

Place a check mark in the *Assigned* column next to the exercises your instructor has assigned to you. Attach this cover sheet to the front of the packet of materials you submit following the laboratory.

Activities	Assigned: Check or list exercise numbers	Completed
Prelab Exercise		
Bridge Exercise		
In-lab Exercise 1		
In-lab Exercise 2		
In-lab Exercise 3		
Postlab Exercise 1		
Postlab Exercise 2		
Total		

Laboratory C: Prelab Exercise

Name _____ Date _____

Section _____

Step 1: Select one of the two methods for acquiring and representing a point in time and use this method to create an implementation of the Timer ADT. Base your implementation on the following class declaration from the file *timer.hs*.

```
// Insert a declaration for SystemTime here.

class Timer
{
  public:

    // Start and stop the timer
    void start ();
    void stop ();

    // Compute the elapsed time (in seconds)
    double getElapsedTime ();

  private:

    SystemTime startTime,   // Time that the timer was started
               stopTime;    // Time that the timer was stopped
};
```

Step 2: Add the appropriate declaration for SystemTime to the beginning of the file and save the resulting header file as *timer.h*. Save your implementation of the Timer ADT in the file *time.cpp*.

Step 3: What is the resolution of your implementation—that is, what is the shortest time interval it can accurately measure?

Laboratory C: Bridge Exercise

Name _____   Date _____

Section _____

Check with your instructor whether you are to complete this exercise prior to your lab period or during lab.

The test program in the program shell file *testc.cs* allows you to test the accuracy of your implementation of the Timer ADT by measuring time intervals of known duration.

```
#include <iostream>
#include <iomanip>
#include <ctime>

#include "timer.h"

using namespace std;

// wait() is cross platform and works well but is not efficient.
// Feel free to replace it with a routine that works better in
// your environment.
void wait(int secs)
{
    int start = clock();
    while (clock() - start < CLOCKS_PER_SEC * secs);
}

void main()
{
    Timer checkTimer;        // Timer
    clock_t timeInterval;    // Time interval to pause

    // Get the time interval.

    // Measure the specified time interval.

    checkTimer.start();           // Start the timer
                                  // Pause for the specified time interval
    checkTimer.stop();            // Stop the timer

    cout << "Measured time interval ( in seconds ) : "
        << checkTimer.getElapsedTime() << endl;
}
```

Step 1: Two data items are left incomplete in this program: the call to the function that pauses the program and the string that prompts the user to enter a time interval. Complete the program by specifying the name of a "pause" function supported by your system. Common names for this function include sleep(), delay(), and pause(). Or you can use the provided wait() function. Add the time unit used by this function to the prompt string. Save the resulting program as *testc.cpp*.

Step 2: Prepare a test plan for your implementation of the Timer ADT. Your test plan should cover intervals of various lengths, including intervals at or near the resolution of your implementation. A test plan form follows.

Step 3: Execute your test plan. If you discover mistakes in your implementation, correct them and execute your test plan again.

Test Plan for the Operations in the Timer ADT

Test Case	Actual Time Period (in seconds)	Measured time period (in seconds)	Checked

Laboratory C: In-lab Exercise 1

Name _____   Date _____

Section _____

In this exercise you will examine the performance of the searching routines in the file *search.cpp*.

Step 1: Use the program in the file *timesrch.cpp* to measure the execution times of the linearSearch(), binarySearch(), and unknownSearch() routines. This program begins by generating an ordered list of integer keys (keyList) and a set of keys to search for in this list (searchSet). It then measures the amount of time it takes to search for the keys using the specified routines and computes the average time per search.

The constant numRepetitions controls how many times each search is executed. Depending on the speed of your system, you may need to use a value of numRepetitions that differs from the value given in the test program. **Before continuing, check with your instructor regarding what value of** numRepetitions **you should use.**

Step 2: Complete the following table by measuring the execution times of the linearSearch(), binarySearch(), and unknownSearch() routines for each of the values of numKeys listed in the table.

Execution Times of a Set of Searching Routines			
Routine	Number of keys in the list (numKeys)		
	1000	2000	4000
linearSearch() O(N)			
binarySearch() O(LogN)			
unknownSearch() O( )			

Step 3: Plot your results below.

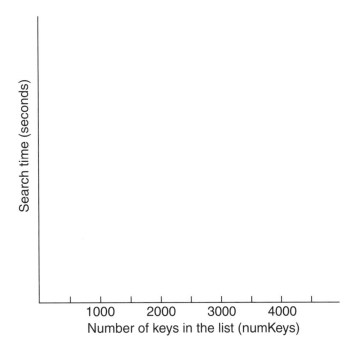

Step 4: How well do your measured times conform with the order-of-magnitude estimates given for the `linearSearch()` and `binarySearch()` routines?

Step 5: Using the code in the file *search.cpp* and your measured execution times as a basis, develop an order-of-magnitude estimate of the execution time of the `unknownSearch()` routine. Briefly explain your reasoning behind this estimate.

Laboratory C: In-lab Exercise 2

Name _____ Date _____

Section _____

In this exercise you will examine the performance of the set of sorting routines in the file *sort.cpp*.

Step 1: Use the program in the file *timesort.cpp* to measure the execution times of the `selectionSort()`, `quickSort()`, and `unknownSort()` routines. This program begins by generating a list of integer keys (`keyList`). It then measures the amount of time it takes to sort this list into ascending order using the specified routine.

The constant `numRepetitions` controls how many times each search is executed. Depending on the speed of your system, you may need to use a value of `numRepetitions` that differs from the value given in the test program. **Before continuing, check with your instructor regarding what value of** `numRepetitions` **you should use.**

Step 2: Complete the following table by measuring the execution times of the `selectionSort()`, `quickSort()`, and `unknownSort()` routines for each combination of the three test categories and the three values of `numKeys` listed in the table.

Execution Times of a Set of Sorting Routines

Routine	Number of keys in the list (numKeys)		
	1000	2000	4000
selectionSort() O(N²)			
quickSort() O(NLogN)			
unknownSort() O( )			

Step 3: Plot your results below.

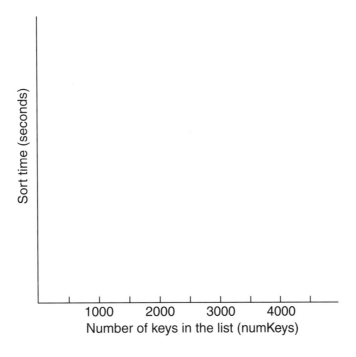

Step 4: How well do your measured times conform with the order-of-magnitude estimates given for the `selectionSort()` and `quickSort()` routines?

Step 5: Using the code in the file *sort.cpp* and your measured execution times as a basis, develop an order-of-magnitude estimate of the execution time of the `unknownSort()` routine. Briefly explain your reasoning behind this estimate.

Laboratory C: In-lab Exercise 3

Name _____   Date _____

Section _____

In this exercise you will measure the performance of the array and linked list implementations of the Stack ADT that you created in Laboratory 5.

Step 1: Using the implementation of the Timer ADT that you created in the Prelab as a foundation, write a program that measures the time it takes to completely fill and then empty a 1000-data item stack using the `push` and `pop` operations in Stack ADT. Because these operations execute so rapidly, you may need to fill and empty the stack a number of times in order to produce an accurate measurement of the time it takes to complete a fill/empty cycle.

Step 2: Use your program to measure the time it takes each of your Stack ADT implementations to fill and empty a stack containing 1000 characters and record the results in the following table.

Step 3: Repeat these measurements using a stack containing 1000 long integers and record the results below.

Time to Fill and Empty a 1000-Data Item Stack		
Stack ADT implementation	Stack data item	
	char	long int
Array implementation		
Linked list implementation		

Laboratory C: Postlab Exercise 1

Name _____   Date _____

Section _____

You are given another pair of searching routines. Both routines have order-of-magnitude execution time estimates of O(N). When you measure the actual execution times of these routines on a given system using a variety of different data sets, you discover that one routine consistently executes five times faster than the other. How can both routines be O(N), yet have different execution times when they are compared using the same system and the same data?

Laboratory C: Postlab Exercise 2

Name _____ Date _____

Section _____

Using your measurements from In-lab Exercises 1 and 2 as a basis, estimate the execution times of the routines listed below for a randomly generated list of 8000 integer keys. Do *not* measure the actual execution times of these routines using a list of this size. Estimate what their execution times will be based on the measurements you have already done. Briefly explain your reasoning behind each estimate.

linearSearch()	Estimated execution time:
Explanation:	

binarySearch()	Estimated execution time:
Explanation:	

selectionSort()	Estimated execution time:
Explanation:	
quickSort()	Estimated execution time:
Explanation:	

Program Validation in C++

Program validation is a very important topic. Much time is wasted because of mistakes on the part of system analysts and programmers. Many of these involve faulty assumptions. The ensuing errors are hard to detect because we often believe to be clearly true something that we have never actually verified. Even worse, we are frequently unaware that we are even making these assumptions. We consequently don't even consider whether or not they might be false. Trying to prove that an entire program is correct is a very complicated formal process that is well beyond the scope of this laboratory book. However, C++ does support two mechanisms—exceptions and assertions—that can be used to validate beliefs at specific points in a program. Including extra statements in your program to validate assumptions may appear to be a lot of effort, but the first time your program triggers an exception or assertion and shows you that something you believed to be absolutely true is in fact false, you will have just saved yourself a tremendous amount of wasted time.

Exceptions

What is an exception? An exception is something you are not expecting to happen. As people we deal with exceptions everyday. For instance, getting into a car accident could be considered a major real-life exception. Hopefully you will never be in a car accident, but if you are, you will likely be very glad that you have insurance and that the people who designed your car included an airbag. When programming, we need to be aware that unexpected events can take place in our programs. The user could type a number when your program expected a letter. You might inadvertently try to allocate more memory than your computer has available. An aardvark might have chewed through your network cable. Any number of ridiculously almost random events could happen to your poor helpless program. You must prepare it. Exceptions allow you to protect you program, to tell it, "This shouldn't happen, but just in case it does ..."

To give you an example from the Logbook ADT—Lab 1—consider what happens if the Logbook constructor is told that it is to initialize the object for month 13, −8, or anything outside of the standard range of months 1 through 12. How should the constructor handle the problem?

- It could go ahead and set the variable `logMonth` to the invalid value, but then everything else goes crazy. If asked to enter information for day 31, should the logbook object complain about an invalid day or not? If asked to print the logbook for the month, how many days does it print? This is reminiscent of the joke about a proposed operating system error message: "File not found. Fake it?" Trying "Number of days in month not known. Wing it?" is not an acceptable solution.
- The function could issue the `return` command to send a warning message to the calling function. This might seem attractive, but there are a number of problems with this. How does a `void` function indicate to the caller that a problem arose? How does a function with a non-`void` return value indicate that the returned value indicates an error situation rather than being valid data? For these and more reasons, using `return` to signal an error does not work well as a general-purpose solution.
- The function could halt the program. This is a radical solution that does not give any other part of the program a chance to try dealing with the problem. Some other part of the program might be able to deal sensibly with the problem, but it never gets a chance. Using the logbook example again, maybe the bad month came from user input. It seems that instead of being forced to halt, it would be better to let the program report the error to the user and ask the user to enter a valid month.
- The program could use exceptions. None of the other approaches to the problem has been very satisfactory, so exceptions became the preferred way for programmers to deal with unexpected error situations.

Many of these situations occur when the code calling a function fails to meet the function's requirements/preconditions. An empty list should not be asked to return the data marked by the cursor. A full list should not be asked to accept more data. The data structure functions should never be called in those situations and should theoretically never have to deal with the problem, but the reality is that functions will get called without proper checking of requirements. So data structures must deal with the possibility of being asked to do unreasonable things.

How do you use exceptions? The basic explanation is simple. When you reach a situation in your code where the function detects a problem that it doesn't have a good way of fixing, you **throw** an exception. **Throwing an exception**—also called **raising an exception**—is the expression used to say that you are telling the program that the local code has encountered a problem so serious that it cannot solve the problem and does not know what to do. Either the calling function, or one of that function's callers, is invited to deal with the problem. Following are the steps for using exceptions in your data structure.

- Include `<stdexcept>` and `<new>` in your C++ program file.
- When your code discovers one of these locally irresolvable problems, throw an exception. The generic syntax is

```
if ( condition ) throw exception_object;
```

where `exception_object` will be one of the standard exceptions defined in `<stdexcept>`. In this lab book, we are using the exception classes

- - logic_error("string exception description"): used to indicate a situation that violates program logic. The code in the program that deals with the exception can access the string and use it to improve error messages and interaction with the user.
  - bad_alloc: used to report a memory allocation failure.
- In the Logbook constructor example, you can deal with an invalid month by writing

```
if ( month < 1 || month > 12 )
    throw logic_error("month not in valid range");
```

There are many other exception classes, but we will not be using them in this book.

- The last step is to declare that the function throws an exception and which exceptions it may throw. This should be done in both the class declaration file—e.g., *logbook.h*—and in the class definition file—e.g., *logbook.cpp*. The syntax is the same for both cases. The Logbook constructor declaration with exception declaration is

```
Logbook ( int month, int year ) throw ( logic_error );
```

When implementing a data structure, throwing an exception as shown above is all that you generally have to do. In the class client code—the code that makes use of the class—you have the choice of whether or not to deal with the exception. If a triggered exception is not dealt with anywhere, then the program is aborted and halts. To deal with an exception, you need a **try block** and a **catch block**. A **code block** is a set of statements joined by a pair of braces—'{' and '}'—into one statement set.

- The try block is used when you are about to call a function that you know may throw an exception. Consider the example of calling the Logbook getEntry() function. You should always take steps to verify that the function parameter meets the requirements, and that is probably enough for something simple like getEntry(). Or, you could be more cautious and try calling getEntry() from within a try block as follows.

```
try
{
    sampleLog.getEntry( userSpecifiedDate );
}
```

- Catch blocks are placed immediately after a try block and are used to specify what to do if the called function does throw an exception. You can either have a catch block set up to catch a specific exception or you can have a general purpose catch block that will catch any exception raised within the preceding try block. For instance, to catch the logic_error exception thrown by getEntry(), you would write something like the following code.

```
catch ( logic_error &e )      // e stands for "exception"
{
    cout << "The date you gave me is not valid for month "
        << sampleLog.getMonth() << endl;
    . . . // Possibly do more to recover from the error
}
```

To catch any error that occurs within the previous try block, you can use a generic catch block like the following.

```
catch ( ... )    // The '...' catches all exception that occur
{
    cout << "The date you gave me is not valid for month "
         << sampleLog.getMonth() << endl;
    . . . // Possibly do more to recover from the error
}
```

You can have multiple catch blocks after a try block. You are in effect overloading the catch block based on the type of the error object thrown.

To summarize what is happening in the previous example, with the try statement we are saying to the compiler, "Watch this code. Look for any exceptions that might occur here." This signals the compiler that exceptions might occur and that we want to do something about them. The throw statement is used to induce an exception. The catch statement that follows the try block tells the compiler what to do if an exception occurs. If we did not have the catch statement in place the exception would be handled by the default handler, which aborts the program.

Until now we have been referring to exceptions as nebulous entities. But what is an exception? C++ allows you to throw any valid data type as an exception. Thus, an exception is just a variable. In the previous example we threw exception objects that are defined in the <stdexcept> header file. However, we could just as well throw an int. C++ then allows you to specify the type of exception that your catch statement will handle. For instance, the following code would catch an exception of type int:

```
catch (int e)
{
    cout << "This is definitely an exception of type int. It's value is:"
         << e << endl;
}
```

The difficulty with throwing exceptions using standard C++ types is that the distinction between different errors within a function is arbitrary. Throwing unique integer values for each type of exception is a workable method for dealing with them. However, keeping track of all the different values that are used to identify the exceptions is a bit of a pain. A better approach is to define a distinct class type for each exception that can occur. This allows the data types themselves to serve as identifiers for the type of exception that has occurred. For the purpose of simplicity in the code in this book, we do not derive exceptions from their base classes.

Note that the discussion above presents a simplified model of how to work with exceptions. It allows us to introduce you to exceptions without being too confusing, and it is sufficient for the purposes of this laboratory book but is by no means complete.

Assertions

The C++ assert statement can be extremely useful during the program development phase. You use it to assert that, at a particular point in your program, something is true. If you are correct, the program continues after checking the assertion—no harm done. However, if you are incorrect, the program stops running and prints a message on the screen showing the assertion that failed and providing the file name and line number in the source code where that assertion occurs.

The syntax details for using assertions are as follows:

- Include the assertion header file by typing

```
#include <cassert>
```

with the other header file inclusion statements.
- Whenever there is something that you believe ought to be true and that you would really want to know about if that belief turned out to be false, type in

```
assert ( bool expression );
```

For instance, if you believe that a variable—call it `temperature`—has a value in a certain range at this point in your program, you could type

```
assert ( temperature >= 80 && temperature <= 90 );
```

If this turns out to be false when the running program encounters this statement, the program will halt with a message similar to the following:

```
weather.exe: main.cpp:9: int main (...):
Assertion 'temperature >= 80 && temperature <= 90' failed.
Aborted
```

Most compilers automatically strip assertions out of the program for distributed production versions of the program. This happens for a number of reasons: Assertions can slow down a program, or they can increase the program size. Also, the end user is often not in a good position to interpret or act on the messages displayed by `assert()`. Finally, it completely halts the running program. Assertions are extremely useful to developers, but they are also best encountered by the developers, not end users.

A Summary of C++ I/O

In our programming experiences we have found that it is often very difficult to find good reference material specifically related to C++ I/O. Rather than pointing a finger toward the library or vaguely gesturing at the Internet, both of which are excellent sources, we have included some reference material that we hope will help you work through the labs in this book. The following is a summary of the standard C++ input and output functions.

I/O Stream State Functions

Method	Returns
rdstate()	The stream state (state)
good()	Nonzero if state is zero; otherwise, returns zero
eof()	Nonzero if eofbit is set; otherwise, returns zero
fail()	Nonzero if failbit is set; otherwise, returns zero
bad()	Nonzero if badbit is set; otherwise, returns zero
clear()	Clears the input status flags (including EOF)

Notes ios States

In the class *ios:* the state variable tracks success/problems in our I/O as follows:

```
class ios {
public:
    ...
    enum io_state {
        goodbit  = 0x00,     // ok -- no bit is set
        eofbit   = 0x01,     // set = eof
        failbit  = 0x02,     // last I/O operation failed
        badbit   = 0x04,     // set = invalid operation
        hardfail = 0x80      // set = unrecoverable error
    };
};
```

A quick way to check whether the status variable for a stream is set to 0 (no flags active) is to say:

```
if ( cin )   // input OK?
{
    whatever ...
}
```

This works because the ios class does some funky operator overloading to return the value of the status variable whenever the name of the stream is used like this in an expression.

The value of `eof()` is not set until a read attempt has been made, so correct usage would be something like:

```
int i;

cin >> i;
while( !cin.eof() )
{
    cout << i << endl;
    cin >> i;
}
```

Operations Available for Opening Files and Streams

Name	Purpose
in	Open for reading
out	Open for writing
ate	Open and move to end-of-stream (*AT E*nd)
app	Open for appending
trunc	Discard stream if it already exists
nocreate	If stream doesn't exist, open fails
noreplace	If stream exists, open for output fails unless *ate* or *app* is set
binary	Open as a binary stream

Notes on File Properties

These are used via the class constructor in two primary ways:

1. When declaring the variable: `fstream var_name( char *name, long flags )`

   (e.g., `fstream my_in_stream( "c:\\junk.dat", ios::in | ios::binary )`)

2. First declaring the variable: `ofstream  my_out_stream;` and then passing the parameters above to the stream open() function.

Another set of useful I/O member functions are for determining/setting your position within a file. The parameters for the second options to seek are `ios::beg` (seek relative to the beginning of the file), `ios::cur` (relative to current pos), and `ios::end` (relative to end of file).

Flags for Formatting Stream Data used with stream.setf(options)

Name	Purpose
skipws	Skip white space
left	Left justify
right	Right justify
internal	Do padding after sign or base flag
dec	Decimal base
oct	Octal base
hex	Hexadecimal
showbase	Show base indicator along with data
showpoint	Print trailing zeros in FP numbers
uppercase	Use uppercase letters for hex output
showpos	Show positive indicator ('+') with positive integers
scientific	Use scientific notation when displaying floating-point numbers
fixed	Use fixed notation for floating-point display
unitbuf	Flush any stream after write
stdio	Flush standard output and std error after write

Useful Stream Methods

Method	Purpose
flags()	Returns a long, which indicates the format flags
flags(long)	Set format flags to the value passed in and return old flags
setf(long)	Set specified flags and return old flags
setf(ios::dec, ios::basefield)	Set integer base to decimal and return old flags
setf(ios::oct, ios::basefield)	Set integer base to octal and return old flags
setf(ios::hex, ios::basefield)	Set integer base to hex and return old flags
setf(ios::left, ios::adjustfield)	Set left justfication and return old flags
setf(ios::right, ios::adjustfield)	Set right justfication and return old flags

Method	Purpose
`setf( ios::internal, ios::internal )`	Put fill char between sign and value and return old flags
`setf( ios::scientific, ios::flatfield )`	Set scientific notation and return the old flags
`setf( ios::fixed, ios::floatfield )`	Set fixed notation and return the old flags
`setf( 0, ios::floatfield )`	Set default notation and return the old flags
`unsetf( long )`	Clear specified flags and return the old flags

Manipulators: Used with Overloaded Input/Output operators >> and <<

Manipulator	Stream	Purpose
`endl`	`ostream`	Write newline and flush stream
`ends`	`ostream`	Write null terminator in string
`flush`	`ostream`	Flush output stream
`ws`	`istream`	Skip white space
`dec`	`ios`	Read/write integers in decimal
`oct`	`ios`	Read/write integers in octal
`hex`	`ios`	Read/write integers in hexadecimal
`setbase( int n )`	`ostream`	Set integer base to n (0 means default)
`setfill( int c )`	`ostream`	Set fill character to c (for padding out fields when we have specified a field width)
`setprecision( int n )`	`ios`	Set precision to n
`setw( int n )`	`ios`	Set field width to n
`setiosflags( long )`	`ios`	Set specified format bits
		(e.g., `setiosflags(ios::showbase | ios::uppercase)`)
`resetiosflags( long )`	`ios`	Clear specified format bits (turn them off)

Methods to Read, Set, and Clear the Format Flag

Name	Behavior
width()	Return field width
width(int)	Set field width to int and return old width (width reverts to 0 after the next number of string is written)
fill()	Return the fill character
fill(char)	Change the fill character and return the old fill char
precision()	Return the precision (num digits in floating-point precision)
precision(int)	Set precision and return old value

Other Miscellaneous Methods

tie(out)	Ties a stream's activities so that out is flushed whenever input is tried by the stream that tied to out.
ios::sync_with_stdio()	Synchronizes C++ I/O with the standard C I/O functions; do this any time you mix usage of both libraries when doing I/O.

Higher-level Methods

Method	Description
`istream& get(signed char*, int, char stop_char)`	Reads characters into buffer pointed to by 1st param, until reach `stop_char` in input or have filled buffer (max char to put in buffer specified by param #2 − 1). An '\0' is placed in the buffer after all other data in the buffer. The `stop_char` is not placed in the buffer and is left in the input stream.
`istream& get( signed char*, int )`	Default `stop_char` is '\n'.
`istream& get( signed char& )`	Read a single character into variable. Reads any/all characters.
`int get()`	Next character in stream. If nothing left, returns EOF.
`istream& read( signed char*, int )`	Like `get`, except that there is no terminator character and no string terminator ('\0') placed in array.
`int gcount()`	Returns the number of characters read by the last read request.
`int peek()`	Returns information about the next character from the stream but doesn't remove it from the stream.
`istream& putback( char )`	Does an 'unget' on a character and puts it back into the input stream to be reread by next request.
`istream& ignore( int count = 1, int stop = EOF )`	Removes count chars from stream or all chars up to stop, whichever is first.
`istream& ignore( int count = 1, int stop = EOF )`	Removes count chars from stream or all chars up to stop, whichever is first.
`istream& putback( char )`	Does an 'unget' on a character and puts it back into the input stream to be reread by next request.
`istream& seekg( streamoff offset, seek_dir dir )`	Set reading position within input stream, `offset` is the byte count of the offset, and `dir` specifies from where (`beg` from beginning of stream, `cur` from current position, and `end` from end of stream). The file should be opened in binary mode when you use this form of the command.
`istream& seekg( streampos pos )`	Set reading position to position `pos` in file. You do not have to be in binary mode to use this.
`streampos tellg()`	Returns the location in the input stream.
`ostream& put( char )`	Place the character in the output stream.
`ostream& write( signed char* buf, int count )`	Count bytes from buffer to output stream.
`ostream& seekp( streamoff, seek_dir )`	Seekg except used for output streams instead of input streams.
`ostream& seekp( streampos )`	Like single-argument version of seekg except used with output streams.
`ostream& tellp()`	Returns the location in the output stream.
`ostream& flush()`	Flushes the buffer—forces stream to actually write out whatever is in the buffer.

Notes on Functions that Return `istream`

All the functions of form `istream& function()` can be used in expressions because the return value gets cast to a zero-value upon failure, or non-zero if the function was successful. This also generally applies to any other functions that return stream pointers (`ifstream`, `ofstream`, etc.).

Notes on fstream-Specific Functions

The constructor is `fstreambase( const char* filename, int mode, int protection = filebuf::openprot )`. The mode is specified by or'ing ios mode bits together (e.g., `ios::out | ios::app`). The protection specifier is usually not specified, so the default value gets used. If the name at least is declared, then the file stream gets opened when it is declared. You would declare a variable to be of type `ifstream` (input file stream), `ofstream` (output file stream), or just `fstream` (input, output, or both), and you can optionally specify the constructor parameters (at declaration time).

If those parameters are not specified when the variable is declared, then the file can be explicitly opened later by using the `open()` member function. The parameters for `open()` are the same as those specified above, and it is used something like `fin.open(name)`. The default for `ifstream` is to open the files in text input mode (`ofstream` opens in text output mode), so if that's what you want you can just go with the default.

There is much more that could be said about these functions, but this will serve as a useful quick reference document for you.

Pointers

A variable can be referenced directly or through one or more levels of indirection: This is where pointers come in. This is especially important with parameter passing for functions.

The size of a pointer depends on the architecture: 32-bit architectures have 32-bit pointers.

& is the unary address operator. It produces the address of its right-hand operand.

* is the unary indirection (or dereferencing) operator. It takes an operand not as a value to use, but as the address of the value to use. This operator can be stacked (e.g., ****cptr).

There are three ways to pass arguments in C++:

- **Call by value:** The value of the operand is placed on the stack and the called function gets a copy of the value, not the original. The called function doesn't even know where the original variable is, so there is no way to modify it. *Note:* Arrays are an exception in that the address of the array is passed instead of the value. This is done for efficiency reasons (and because too many people would keep blowing the stack by trying to pass too much data around on it).
- **Call by reference:** Reference arguments are like aliases. To specify that a parameter is passed by reference, place an ampersand ('&') in front of the variable name in the prototype and function declaration. The compiler takes care of all the work so that when the variable is used in the local function, the original variable gets updated. *Note:* You can create reference variables for use as aliases within a function, not just as parameters.
- **Call by address:** The value passed is the address of the data structure we need to deal with, not the value of the data structure. Consequently, all references to that data structure will require the dereferencing operator *. *Note:* An astute observer may point out that a call by address is actually a call by value in which the value is a memory address. This is true. We make the distinction here only for sake of explanation.

Using library (and other) functions, you will often see a function declaration that looks something like the following:

```
char *func_1(int request, struct *sptr, int &orig)
```

To use this function, you must understand what parameters the function is expecting. The first parameter must be passed by value. The second one expects a call by address with a pointer argument, and all uses of it within the function will use the `*` dereferencing operator. The third is a call by reference with reference arguments and will be treated syntactically like a call by value (no dereferencing or anything—the compiler takes care of that).

Pointer and Array Equivalence

Pointers and arrays are pretty much interchangeable in C/C++. This is a bit confusing, but here's the basic idea:

An array is nothing more than a base address of a series of data items. So if I declare an array `int my_ints[SOME_NUMBER]`, what I really have is a pointer to the base address of where the array is located in memory (`my_ints` is the pointer), knowledge about the size of each item (in this case `sizeof (int)`), and an idea of how many items (`SOME_NUMBER`) of that data type will have had memory allocated for them by the compiler. To reference the third item I could type `my_ints[2]`, or I could type `*( my_ints + 2 )`; they are completely equivalent. In the second example we are doing what is called pointer math. The compiler takes the address of the pointer and adds 2 * the sizeof `int`. The basic array indexing scheme is to take the address of the array pointer (the base address) and add the value `index * element_size`. This gives us the offset. So, you see that arrays do not really exist in C/C++, but we can act as though they do. Multidimension arrays can also be converted to pointers, though that is a bit more confusing. Consult your textbook for details.

A function parameter `int myints[]` gets converted to `int * const myints`, which is read as myints is a constant pointer to an integer. There are several possible combinations of `const` with pointers.

- `const int * ptr` — This is read: `ptr` is a pointer to a constant integer. This means that what it points at cannot be changed (the integer is constant), but the pointer itself can be changed (it can be set to point at something else, though it still can't be used for changing values). Using this helps avoid accidentally changing data you are using.

- `int * const ptr` — This is read: `ptr` is a constant pointer to an integer. This means that we can change what the pointer is pointing at (e.g., `*ptr = something`), but cannot make the pointer point somewhere else (the pointer is constant).

- `const int * const ptr` — This is read: `ptr` is a constant pointer to a constant integer. We can neither change the data pointed at nor where the pointer is pointing.

- `int * ptr` — Just for completeness, `ptr` is a pointer to integer. Both the data pointed at and where the pointer points can be modified.

It is good software engineering practice to give a function only as much access to data as it absolutely needs. The results are more complicated-looking code, but it can save tons of time that otherwise would be spent debugging to determine how and where something was getting magically changed. So if a function uses an array but doesn't need to change the data, it would be best passed as `const type * ptr`, or even `const type * const ptr`.

Pointer math: Pointers can be incremented (++) and decremented (--), integers can be added or subtracted from pointers (+, +=, −, -=) or one pointer may be subtracted from another. The general rule to remember is that the arithmetic is always done in terms of the size of the data type pointed at. For example, `ptr += 2` means "change what we are pointing at by 2 * sizeof the data type"; if the datatype is 8 bytes, then ptr now points 2 * 8 = 16 bytes higher. `ptr2 − ptr1` gives you the difference between the two pointers as a difference between the array index value of `ptr2` and `ptr1`, so if `ptr2` points to `array[3]` and `ptr1` points to `array[1]`, `ptr2 − ptr1 = 2` (since the `ptr2` points to an element two elements away from `ptr1`). Pointer math only makes sense in the context of an array.

C-Strings: C-strings are just pointers to an array of characters. The string end is calculated by starting at item 0 in the array and moving up through the indexed characters until a character with the value '\0' is found; that is the end of the string. *Note:* There is a big difference between an empty string (the first item in the array has the value '\0') and a null string (the pointer has the value NULL, or `(char *) 0`). A NULL pointer by our definition doesn't point at any data.